FRESCO PAINTING

FRESCO PAINTING
for home & garden

Sarah Hocombe

David & Charles

A DAVID & CHARLES BOOK

First published in the UK in 1999 by David & Charles

Text © 1999 Sarah Hocombe
Volume © 1999 Breslich & Foss Ltd

A catalogue record for this book is available from the British Library.

ISBN 0 7153 0838 6

This book was conceived by
Breslich & Foss Ltd
20 Wells Mews
London W1 3FJ

Project manager: Janet Ravenscroft
Designer: Ruth Prentice
Photographer: Shona Wood
Templates: Anthony Duke

Printed and bound by C.S. Graphics Pte Ltd.

For David & Charles
Brunel House
Newton Abbot
Devon

SAFETY NOTE
Care must be taken
to follow the
suggested
precautions at all
times when
handling dry
pigments and lime.
Neither the author
nor the publishers
can be held
responsible for any
consequences of
mishandling the
materials used in
this book.

The publishers would like to thank the following picture agencies for
permission to reproduce photographs: The Ancient Art and Architecture
Collection, page 22; SCALA pages 34, 43, 56, 80-81, 88, 116-117.

CONTENTS

INTRODUCTION

This book is offered as an introduction to the traditional fresco technique, a method of wall painting that has been practised continuously for thousands of years. The projects have been selected because they explore a variety of techniques and different styles. It is hoped that they will provide inspiration for further experimentation.

The fresco painting technique is a simple one. Pure lime-proof pigments are mixed with water and painted onto a fine layer of fresh, damp, lime plaster that has been spread onto a wall or panel. As it dries, a chemical reaction takes place which produces calcium carbonate crystals on the surface of the plaster. The pigments are fixed in this hard crystalline layer. This process of carbonisation will continue for a long time and, as a result, the colour in a fresco gradually become richer and deeper, rather than fading as in other painting techniques. The painting, not a surface decoration, but an integral part of the wall, will last as long as the plaster surface itself. A well-executed fresco painting, therefore, possesses unsurpassed luminosity and durability – qualities which have fascinated both artists and art lovers throughout the centuries.

Because the painting must be completed while the plaster is still damp, large-scale or detailed work is executed in sections. Only one section is completed at a time and then fresh plaster is applied to the next area to be painted. The plaster will remain damp for about a day and each section of painting is therefore called a *giornata* from the Italian for day. The colours used are those that are resistant to the alkalinity of the lime. The fresco palette, therefore, has remained fairly consistent over millennia and many of the pigments used today are the same as those that were used by the Minoans, Etruscans and Romans. In Renaissance frescoes, such as Gozzoli's Chapel of the Magi, colours were added after the plaster was dry, using

pigment mixed with a binding medium such as egg. The use of the egg tempera technique is demonstrated in this book.

Today there is a resurgence of interest in building with lime mortar and this may provide opportunities for more large-scale fresco paintings to be executed. Yet whether on a large or small scale, fresco continues to enchant practitioners and viewers alike.

MATERIALS AND
TECHNIQUES

This book demonstrates the use of the professional fresco technique that has been practised by master artists and craftspeople for thousands of years. In the past, practitioners would have used good studio practice, and today there are still a number of health and safety precautions to be taken. Set out below are important guidelines for the sensible use of pigments and lime, the two main ingredients of fresco painting. These materials are not suitable for children to use; make sure that they are carefully stored and that children do not come into contact with them.

PLASTER

In all but one of the projects in this book (the Tiger), only two coats of plaster are used. The painting layer is referred to as top-coat plaster and the layer onto which it is applied as base-coat plaster. The plaster is made from a mixture of lime putty and sharp washed sand in proportions that change depending on whether you are mixing the top-coat or base-coat layer.

Lime putty is made by 'slaking', or immersing in water, quicklime. It can be bought in tubs, either from specialist decorating or art shops or firms specialising in supplying materials to the conservation or lime mortar building trade. Lime putty for fresco should have been slaked for at least six months. The older the lime putty, the better its quality will be: unslaked particles of lime can affect the painting badly, splitting off and causing spotting, sometimes months after the painting has been completed. For this reason, professional fresco artists sieve the putty before use by pushing it through a fine mesh with a decorator's brush. Tubs of putty should be kept well sealed to prevent the lime from drying out, and should be protected from frost.

Lime putty is caustic, so always wear old clothes and waterproof gloves when handling it. When decanting the putty from its tub you are particularly at risk from splashes of lime water or putty, so wear protective goggles. These will also ensure that you do not accidentally rub your eyes with your gloved hand. The mixed lime plaster is also caustic and should not be allowed to come into contact with your eyes, mouth or skin (cuts are particularly susceptible to burns from the lime). Use barrier cream and/or gloves when plastering.

PLASTER RECIPES

Base-coat plaster mix
2 parts fine sharp washed dry sand and 1 part mature lime putty, laid about 1cm (½in) thick.

Top-coat plaster mix
1 part fine sharp washed dry sand and 1 part mature lime putty, laid 3-5mm (¼in) thick.

Only sharp sand is suitable for fresco plaster. Kiln-dried washed sharp sand is available from some builder's merchants, but it is best to test a batch by washing it and looking for signs of dirt or debris before using it. The sand's colour will determine the dry colour of the plaster.

Mixing the plaster

Add sand to the lime putty and mix with a trowel. As you mix the sand and putty together the plaster will become more and more pliable and moist. A stiffer plaster is harder to mix than a wet one, but don't give in to the temptation to add water: it will weaken the plaster by increasing its rate of shrinkage and making it liable to crack. Add a little more putty if the plaster is still dry and crumbly after thorough mixing. When it sticks to the trowel and adheres well to the support it is ready to use. When the plaster mix is right, it should ideally be left to 'rest' overnight then mixed again before use. Store plaster in sealed waterproof containers, or wrapped up well in plastic.

The proportions given for the plaster recipes are a general guide and you may need to adjust them slightly; the exact amount of putty to sand depends on the

type of sand you are using and the moisture content of the putty. Always measure the quantities accurately: use a container such as an empty yoghurt pot to add full level measures of putty and sand. Keep track of what you add to the mix by noting it down. As well as helping to make sure you are following a guide recipe correctly, this will provide useful reference for the future.

It is advisable to experiment with a few plaster mixes before embarking on your first fresco. Try mixing up a small batch of top-coat plaster using exactly the quantities given in the recipe. If it seems too dry or runny, make up a second batch, adjusted accordingly.

Well-mixed top-coat plaster, with the right stiff, slightly sticky consistency.

Make a third and fourth sample: one that seems very dry, the other seemingly too wet and apply them to a terracotta tile that has been soaked in water for at least two hours. Spread one sample on each of the four quarters of the tile. Keep the remainder of the batches wrapped in plastic. When the tile is dry, you will be able to judge which plaster worked best, cracking least and offering the best painting surface. Refer to the wet reserved sample as a guide for mixing future batches with the same sand and putty.

SUPPORTS

Some plaster samples: top left is a tile with a 'floated' surface. The tile next to it has a 'trowelled' surface; the difference in colour is due to the sand used. The plaster on the tile at bottom left has cracked because the mix was too wet. The tile next to it was plastered with lime putty mixed with marble dust, which creates a very white surface.

The top layer of plaster, onto which the fresco is painted, needs to remain damp for as long as possible. In order to achieve this, the top-coat plaster must be applied over a deep absorbent ground, which has first been thoroughly dampened with water. This moist base allows the top coat to dry gradually, thereby extending the painting time and allowing thorough carbonisation of the colours. It also helps to prevent cracks forming. While the principle of creating a moist ground remains the same, there are several different types of support suitable for fresco painting.

Wooden panels

A layer of expanding metal lath, known as EML (available from builder's merchants) can be fixed to a panel with masonry nails then coated with base-coat plaster. The panel should be made of a wood which will not warp and cause the plaster to crack. Marine-quality plywood and MDF are suitable. A board 13mm (½in) thick is sufficient for a small panel, whilst larger pieces should be made of thicker, 2cm (¾in) board. Making panels larger than about 1.2m (4ft) square is impractical, due to the weight of the plaster.

The shallow cups, or lugs, in the EML trap the plaster.

Wear protective gloves when cutting EML. If possible, cut where two lugs meet creating two smooth edges. If the size of the panel means that you have to cut down the middle of a lug, try to keep smooth edges on the outside so that you don't have sharp points sticking out from the edge of the panel. Attach the EMl to the surface with masonry nails. Start in the centre and work outwards, top and bottom, left and right, applying the nails in a diamond pattern.

Lightly spray the panel with water then plaster the surface with base-coat plaster mix. First look closely at the EML. You will see that the lugs are like shallow cups. These

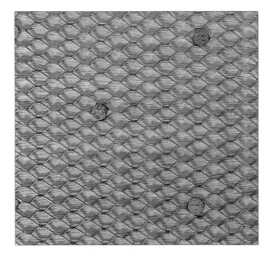

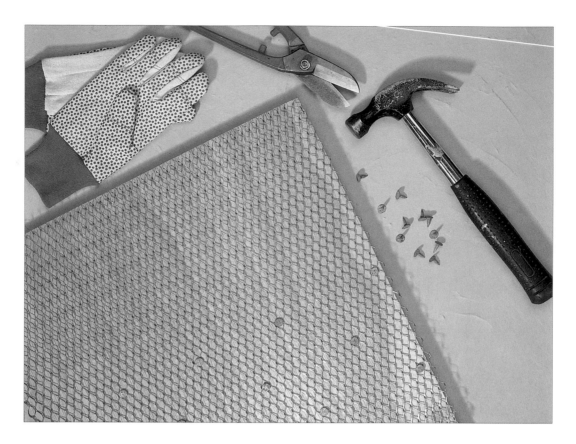

Line up the EML with the edges of the board and attach it with masonry nails. If you are going to attach the finished piece to the wall, apply the fixings to the back of the board at this stage.

should be filled up with plaster by pulling the trowel firmly over the surface, forcing the plaster into the cups (if you trowel the plaster on in the wrong direction you will not be able to fill them). Having filled the lugs, cover the whole surface to a further depth of 2 or 3mm ($\frac{1}{16}$ to $\frac{1}{8}$ in). At this point the surface will have been roughly smoothed with the trowel. Rub over the surface with the wooden or sponge float using a circular motion. (You may have to wait twenty minutes or so, until the plaster is firm enough.) This will give the plaster a slight 'tooth'. Allow this ground to dry thoroughly before dampening it to use as a support for top-coat plastering.

Terracotta tiles

Small frescoes can be painted on plaster laid onto a terracotta support. Thick tiles, such as floor tiles and some roofing tiles are suitable. As with other supports, a tile needs to hold water in order to keep the painting layer of plaster damp for as long as possible. The thicker the tile, the better support it will be. Most tiles will have a key on their underside, such as ridges or a rough texture. This is the side onto which the plaster should be applied. Ideally, tiles should be soaked overnight, or for at least a couple of hours before plastering. If the tile is still 'thirsty', it will draw moisture down from the plaster, drying it out too quickly and causing cracks to form. Any water droplets should be wiped from the surface before applying the plaster, which can either be top coat alone, or base coat then top coat.

Brick walls

The traditional fresco support is a brick wall, pointed with lime mortar, or a stone wall, onto which three coats of plaster are laid. The method is described in detail in the large-scale Tiger project on page 122 but, in essence, a first coat of rough lime plaster is laid and left to dry. It is then dampened and a second coat of plaster is laid on top of it and allowed to dry. Having been dampened down again, the painting layer, made of 1 part lime putty mixed with about 1 part sand is applied.

Hessian

Hessian can be used as a support for a thin layer of top-coat plaster. As it can be stuck to existing painted walls, it is useful for work that has to be painted in places where preparation of a deep ground is not possible. The plaster dries quickly so working on hessian is most suitable for small pieces and simple compositions. The method is fully described on page 116, the Roman Fragments project.

PLASTERING TECHNIQUES

Applying the base coat

When you have prepared a support, use a trowel to apply the plaster in a layer about 1cm (⅜in) thick. The trowel should be slightly flexible and have a rounded point. For very small pieces such as tiles, a large diamond-shaped palette knife with a round point can be used. Press the plaster firmly onto the surface. At this stage, concentrate on achieving an even layer; do not worry about creating a smooth surface. If you see any air bubbles under the surface pop them with a needle then flatten the plaster. When the plaster is firm enough (you may have to wait twenty minutes or so), rub over the whole of the surface with a sponge or wooden float to give it a slight 'tooth'. The float is used with a circular motion. When you float the surface you may notice areas that need more plaster added to bring them up to the same height as the rest. These should be filled with blobs of plaster from the trowel then floated. The surface is left with this rough 'floated' surface, which supplies a key for the top-coat plaster. This ground should be allowed to dry slowly over a few days before being dampened and used as a support for top-coat plastering.

When you are satisfied that the base coat is dry, use a plant spray or decorator's brush to dampen the surface thoroughly. Allow the water to be absorbed, then repeat until water remains on the surface; this is the sign that the dry plaster has taken in all the moisture it can. Blot off any surface water with an absorbent cloth then apply the top-coat plaster.

Applying the top coat

Thoroughly dampen the base coat then apply the top-coat plaster in a layer of between 3 and 5mm (⅛ and ¼in) thick. Rather than leaving the plaster rough when you have floated it as you did for the base coat, smooth it with the trowel. This is done with light pressure, first over the whole surface in one direction then in the opposite one (that is, at right angles to the first pass). Continue until the plaster is smooth, being careful to use the trowel lightly, not working over one spot for too long or with too much pressure.

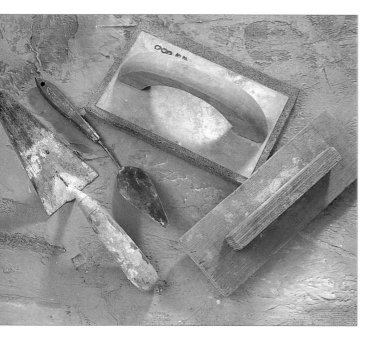

The top-coat plaster is painted on while still damp (see **Stages of Painting**). The drying rate of this layer will vary depending on the depth of the ground onto which it is laid, the air temperature and the amount of moisture in the atmosphere. Generally, it will be reasonably dry after about a week, but the carbonisation process will go on for a long time, the painting first changing dramatically then subtly in appearance as the process continues. Depending on the depth of the plaster base coats, the painting will arrive at something close to its final state after six months to a year.

Basic plastering tools from left to right: trowel, palette knife, sponge float and wooden float.

If possible, plaster should be allowed to dry away from direct sunlight and breezes, both of which may dry it out too quickly, causing cracks. Tiles dry more slowly if they have a plastic bag or plastic sheet laid beneath them to prevent evaporation from the back. To slow down drying times in a warm climate, tiles and other small panels can be covered with plastic, but make sure that the plastic does not touch the soft, damp plaster surface. If necessary, larger pieces can also be covered with plastic sheeting or damp sacking. Again, ensure that the soft painted surface is protected.

Repairs

If a painting has been damaged it is best repaired with some of the original plaster, but if this is not possible, mix up the necessary quantity of a roughly approximate mix. Rake out any loose material from the damaged piece with the point of a trowel. Dampen down the area thoroughly, concentrating on the area to be filled or replaced: too much water on the painted surface may cause staining. Plaster as usual then paint in the missing areas with the original colours. If this is not possible, use matching colours that you have tested.

PREPARING THE DESIGN

A design is transferred to the painting surface in one of two ways. In the first, pigment is dusted through pierced holes made in the design, in the second a point is used to score the outline onto the plaster. Designs for both methods should be prepared on tracing paper or, for larger compositions, onto something more robust and water-resistant, such as parcel wrapping paper.

Patterns are supplied at the back of this book and should be enlarged to fit the tile or panel you are decorating. It is easiest to do this on a photocopier, but if one is not available, the enlargement can be achieved by 'squaring up'. To do this, trace the design in the book and draw a series of squares onto it. Take a piece of paper the size of the finished project and draw squares onto it in the same proportion and position as those on your tracing taken from the book. If the design from the book is divided into sixteen squares, for example, the piece of paper should be divided up into sixteen squares, the divisions falling at the same point (half way up, a quarter of the way up, and so forth) on the full size paper, as on the design in the book. Copy out the lines within each square onto the full size design. If the design is a complicated one, it helps to number the squares. The same method is used to enlarge designs for mural paintings (see page 122).

Pouncing

Pouncing is the most suitable way to transfer small-scale work and details of larger compositions to the plaster. Place the prepared design face down on a soft surface, such as a folded blanket or towel. Use a needle to prick through holes about 5mm (¼in) apart (for details holes can be so close together as to form an almost continuous line). The design should be pricked through from the back because the points created on the surface of the paper by piercing can make indentations on the plaster surface. Push the needle through far enough to make a distinct round hole. You may prefer to mount the needle into a handle; an empty propelling pencil of the sort that grips the lead with its 'jaws' is useful.

Pouncing the design onto the surface should be done when the plaster is ready to paint (see **Stages of Painting**). If the design is pounced on too soon, the dots of pigment will be indistinct. Lay the design on the surface and dust the pigment through with a soft mop brush, such as a goat's hair one, or a pounce bag. Working with a brush is most suitable for horizontal panels. If the panel is vertical, the design should be held in position with small nails or masking tape.

A pounce bag can be bought or made from two small squares of fine muslin, into the centre of which a spoonful of pigment is placed. The muslin is then tied into a bag by pulling up its corners, holding them together and wrapping string round and round the neck of the bag then tying it off.

In order to get the clearest outline possible, gently press the design down, holding it close to the plaster surface. Use as little pigment as is necessary to give a clear impression; check whether you are using the right amount, by lifting up a corner of the design soon after starting to pounce.

If the composition involves a lot of fine detail, join up the dots of pigment when you have finished pouncing. Use a wash of the pouncing pigment and a fine brush. (Colours for pouncing are listed with the projects.) The reason for doing this is that the dots of pigment will be fixed by the plaster as it dries and left as small insoluble mounds.

When pouncing, the greatest care possible must be taken not to inhale any pigment dust, or get it into your eyes or on your skin.

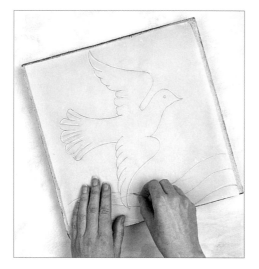

The design is scored through with a nail.

Scoring through

The alternative method of transferring the design to the surface is to place the drawn design, without any pricking through, onto the damp plaster, face up. With a small nail or blunt pencil, trace over the main lines of the composition, using enough pressure to leave a shallow indentation in the surface. The advantage of scoring through is that the indentations do not disappear when they are painted over and so it is easy to keep track of the guide outlines. This is particularly useful when painting in washes that would lift off a pounced outline.

This method is not suitable for very fine work because it does not reproduce detail very clearly. The indentations in the surface can also become visually distracting on a small panel. Sometimes, if a piece is displayed for a long time the dents can trap dust, becoming more and more noticeable.

FRESCO PIGMENTS

Many of the pigments used today for fresco painting have been used for thousands of years. In different eras and different civilisations the core colours remained the same. The Minoans, Greeks, Romans, Indian artists and European painters of the Middle Ages and Italian Renaissance all used native iron oxides for their reds and yellows. Iron oxide and lamp blacks were used in Roman times. Lime putty has always been used for white, though in Renaissance times Bianco Sangiovanni, a white prepared from lime putty was used.

The blue pigments used in fresco have changed over the centuries. The ancestor of our cobalt blue and cerulean blues is Egyptian blue. As its name implies, this

Colours change quite dramatically depending on whether they are combined with white, and the sort of white used. Here's an example using cobalt blue light.

Pure cobalt blue light.

Cobalt blue light mixed with marble dust.

Cobalt blue light mixed with lime putty.

Cobalt blue light mixed with titanium white.

Cobalt blue light mixed with blanc fixe (barium sulphate).

colour originated in ancient Egypt. The Minoans imported the colour (or learnt how to prepare it from the Egyptians). It was used by the Etruscans and Romans. Today it can be imitated with cobalt blue light, sometimes tinted with cerulean or a little green. Cobalt blue was introduced as a painting pigment in the 1820s and cerulean in the 1870s. During the Italian Renaissance, lapis lazuli was ground to produce ultramarine – then the costliest of pigments – which was applied to fresco in a binder when it was dry. Today artificial ultramarine, introduced as a pigment in the 1820s is sometimes used in fresco, though there is some controversy about its suitability. Pigment suppliers should be able to advise you about the suitability of the ultramarine they supply.

Copper-based greens, green earth and greens mixed from Egyptian blue and green earth are traditional to fresco. Viridian was introduced as a pigment in the 1850s and chromium oxide green in the 1860s.

Lime-proof pigments

Frescoes have been painted for thousands of years, and are not famous for provoking illness in their creators, but it is, nevertheless, extremely important to follow sound studio practice when using dry pigments. All fine dusts pose a health risk and there is a possibility that persistent exposure may cause you harm. If you are pregnant, or considering becoming pregnant seek medical advice before working with pigments in powder form.

Try to establish a dedicated working area for painting frescoes, and wear working clothes that you wash frequently. Don't cook with utensils that you have used to handle any fresco ingredients. Keep work areas clean: clean up spills well with damp paper towels and vacuum thoroughly, disposing carefully of waste. When handling large quantities of dry pigments wear an approved mask/respirator (check with your supplier for details of the relevant level of protection). Don't work near a draught or fan that will blow dust about, and don't eat, drink or smoke in the work area: you risk transferring pigment dust to your mouth. Protect your hands and skin, making sure that cuts or abrasions are not exposed to pigment dust. Keep your hands away from your face and eyes and wash them frequently, remembering to clean under your nails.

Ask your supplier for advice on the safest handling of the pigments they supply and follow it scrupulously. Some suppliers can provide pigments in paste form, and you may wish to use these as an alternative to dry powdered pigments. However, first check that they are suitable for fresco.

Using lime-proof pigments is essential in fresco painting. A list of the pigments used in the projects in this book is given opposite, but there are other colours suitable for using in lime. Store pigments in sealed, unbreakable containers. If your pigment is supplied in bags, they should be cut open (not untied) and decanted into storage jars. Putting the bag directly into a container, or removing the pigment with a spoon or scoop is best; pouring out the pigment creates dust.

It is important to test all the colours before you use them, for two reasons. First, pigments should be tested for lime-fastness. Unless you can be absolutely sure of its chemical composition (some suppliers will give you this information), it is impossible to be a hundred per cent sure that a pigment is going to resist the alkalinity of the lime. The second reason for testing colours is to become familiar with their appearance when painted and dried.

Preparation of colours

The pigments used in fresco are mixed with water and stored in air-tight jars in paste form. Secondary colours are mixed from these pastes. More water is added to the paste to dilute it for mixing or painting. The colours are generally used in a watery state, the consistency of milk. The water used can either come directly from the tap or be distilled water, cooled boiled water, or lime water.

Distilled water or cooled boiled water should be free from mineral impurities and lower in bacteria than tap water, so I would recommend using these to prepare pigment pastes and colours that are to be stored for any length of time. Lime water, the water on the top of the container of putty, can give the colours a slightly chalky appearance if care is not taken to allow all the fragments of lime to settle out of it.

COLOURS USED IN THIS BOOK

White: *lime putty, titanium white*

Blue: *ultramarine*, cobalt blue light (also called cobalt blue pale; substitute with cobalt blue dark mixed with titanium white if unavailable), cobalt blue dark, cerulean*

Earth reds: *burnt sienna, Venetian red, red earth, Herculaneum earth (substitute with the brightest, yellowish red earth colour you can find if unavailable)*

Pink: *cinabrese (substitute by mixing 1 part burnt sienna and 4 parts titanium white if unavailable)*

Yellow: *raw sienna, yellow ochre, Mars yellow*

Green: *green earth, viridian, chromium oxide, bright green (any bright green artificial lime-proof colour; it will be sold under a number of different names)*

Violet: *caput mortum (also called 'morellone')*

Black: *either an iron oxide black, such as Mars black, or lamp black*

Brown: *burnt umber, raw umber*

Graphite and mica flakes: *each of these glitter pigments is used in one project only*

*Please note that artificial ultramarine is considered by some practitioners to be stable in lime, and by others not to be. It is definitely susceptible to acids and therefore not appropriate for outdoor use. As it is a cheap pigment, I have suggested its use for the coloured plaster mixes, but with the proviso that it should be tested before use.

To prepare a colour, spoon the dry pigment into a jar, add water and stir carefully. When the pigment has a paste-like consistency, pour a little more water into the jar so that it forms a layer about 13mm (½in) thick. This sits on top of the pigment and stops it drying out.

For secondary mixes, pour off the water sealing the paste and remove the given quantity of paste with a spoon or palette knife. Place in another jar with the other colour pastes. Add more water to thin the colour to a milky consistency. The contents of the jar should then be stirred or, alternatively, shaken with the lid of the jar in place. If the paint is too thick, it will sit proud of the surface and will not be fixed by the plaster. Label all jars with their colour recipe or content.

Colour testing

Colours should initially be tested to see whether they are lime proof. Do this by painting them out onto a prepared terracotta tile and allowing them to dry. To test colour mixes, paint them onto a tile, either writing the proportions of the mix directly onto the tile, or numbering the tests and keeping a record of the colour recipes on paper. The tile will have to dry for about a week before you can judge what the final appearance of the colour is to be, so it is best to test all the variations of the colour you think will work at the same time.

PIGMENTS

In the instructions for **Pre-mixed pigments**, *1 tsp means one level teaspoon of pigment paste. You will find that small quantities of pigment are referred to as pigments* **On the palette**. *Taking out blobs of colour from your main jar when you are about to use them is best, but if you find that they dry out too quickly, use small quantities of dry colour as a last resort.*

STAGES OF PAINTING

Clockwise from top left: *test tile with unmixed pigments (i.e. not combined with other colours); dry pigments, including mica and graphite; tile with mixed colour tests; dry pigments; palette knife used to lift pigment from pots; pots with lids for storing pigment pastes and mixed colours.*

The plaster is ready to be painted on when you can touch it quite firmly with a fingertip without leaving a discernible impression. Another test is to draw a brush loaded with water lightly across the surface of the plaster. The brush shouldn't score the surface and the water transferred to it should be absorbed quite quickly by the plaster. This indicates that the plaster is 'thirsty' enough to accept paint. This moment may come at anything between twenty minutes and a few hours after plastering, depending on the support, atmospheric conditions and the plaster used, so it is important to test the surface regularly.

Washes of dilute colour are applied in the early stages of the painting and, if necessary, can be blurred with a soft brush such as a sable fan brush or goat's hair softening brush. When the plaster is drier, it 'drinks' the colour so quickly that it does not remain on the surface long enough to be softened. Use the brush very lightly, without disturbing the surface of the plaster. Churning up the surface, apart from creating unwanted texture, mixes the lime with the colour, lightening it considerably.

When the plaster surface is thirsty enough to absorb the colour almost instantly, you can paint opaque strong colours, lines and fine details. This is a magical time, when you can paint quickly and deftly. Work confidently, making the most of the time the plaster allows you. Remember not to apply the paint too thickly: it may clog the ground. When the colour is no longer being fixed by the hardening plaster, it is time to stop working. To get a feel for painting times, paint on prepared terracotta tiles. Paint the same design with the same colours, a number of times, at different stages of the plaster's life. When all are dry, compare their appearance. Wash the surface of the tiles gently with water and see whether any of the pigment remains unfixed.

The difference between a wet and a dry fresco is generally quite dramatic. This is because the plaster becomes much lighter and more reflective as it dries. Brushstrokes tend to become more visible against this light tone than they were on the mid-tone of the wet plaster. In the early stages of drying, the colours can appear quite uneven and patchy, but even out as the plaster dries, becoming paler but at the same time more luminous as the carbonisation process continues.

BRUSHES

Many different brushes are suitable for use in fresco. Bear in mind that the lime will dry out the bristles and that after some use they will become stiff and will no longer be suitable for other sorts of painting. Synthetic brushes are more resistant

to the lime. Soft bristled brushes are best; the harder ones will score the surface of the plaster. I tend to use goat's hair flats and mops for softening; sables, squirrel hair or soft hair acrylic brushes for fine lines, and ox hair flats for large areas. Experiment with what is available, remembering that when the plaster is really wet only the softest brushes are suitable, whilst as it hardens, progressively stiffer bristles can be used (some of the traditional fresco brushes are made from soft hog's hair). Wash brushes with water and, if possible, a neutral olive oil soap. Do not use detergent: it will dry the bristles out further.

When painting straight lines, you might find it helpful to rest your hand on a mahlstick, which can be bought at art and crafts shops, or made at home.

Anti-clockwise from centre left: a mahlstick; flat soft hair brushes (the three on the left are oxhair, the last is synthetic); various sizes of pointed soft hair brushes, sable and synthetic; a traditional 'fresco' brush; goat's hair softening brushes and a sable, fan-shaped softener; three lining fitches, used with a ruler for painting straight lines; a soft hair filbert-shaped brush that can be used as a substitute for a lining fitch; three riggers, used for painting long lines; four squirrel hair brushes.

THE
PROJECTS

MINOAN FISHERMAN

From the West House at Akrotiri, Santorini

This graceful figure of a young man returning with his catch was painted on the island of Thera (now Santorini), in Greece, between 1550 and 1500 BC. The painting adorned the wall of a patrician family home and it has been suggested that it is a portrait of the son of the owner of the house.

This fresco is in the Minoan style, characterised by a great sense of delight in nature and spontaneous bold brushwork. The painter has drawn the figure with a fluid outline which, despite his rather formal pose, gives the fisherman a great sense of movement. The fish have each been given different expressions, making them more vibrant and lively as a result.

When working from a Minoan original, or creating a work in the spirit of Minoan painting, capturing the fluid outline of the figures and major forms is the key to success. A flowing, unbroken line works better than a line that becomes hesitant or broken as a result of trying to follow the guide line too carefully. Here, the finished piece was fixed to a wall with mirror plates and plaster applied around it.

MATERIALS

30 x 45cm (1ft x 1½ft) board coated with EML and approx. 1.6kg (3½lb) base-coat plaster mix and 1.1kg (2½lb) top-coat plaster mix

♦

Pounce bag or soft mop brush

♦

Palette

♦

Small sea sponge

♦

Brushes: 2.5cm (1in) flat soft hair, goat's hair softener, no. 10 soft hair pointed, no. 0 soft hair pointed

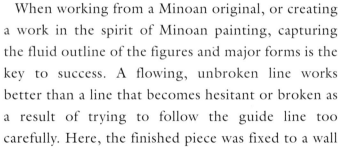

PIGMENTS

Pre-mixed

Background: *1 tsp yellow ochre, 1 tsp titanium white, ½ tsp red earth*

Blue stripe, fishes' backs, 'hat': *1 tsp cerulean blue, ½ tsp green earth, ¼ tsp burnt umber, ¼ tsp white combined*

Yellow stripe, fishes' bellies, necklace, rope: *1 tsp yellow ochre*

Brown stripe: *¼ tsp burnt umber, ¼ tsp red earth combined*

Dark stripe at base of panel: *¼ tsp black, ¼ tsp burnt umber, ¼ tsp cerulean combined*

Body: *1 tsp Herculaneum earth, 1 tsp red earth*

On the palette *a little black, titanium white and burnt umber*

Pigment for pouncing the design
½ tsp green earth

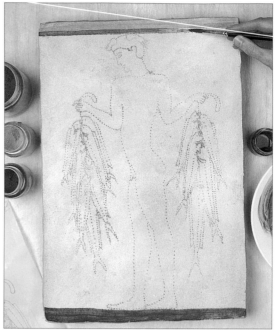

1 When the plaster is ready for painting, mix up dilute washes of yellow ochre, titanium white and red earth. 'Dirty' the washes on the palette with a touch of burnt umber. Use the 2.5cm (1in) brush to apply the washes in patches on the surface then blur them immediately with the goat's hair softening brush. Keep the colours very light; they will show up a lot more when the plaster has dried.

2 Pounce through the design with green earth then paint in the three stripes at the top of the panel and the one at the bottom using the pre-mixed colours.

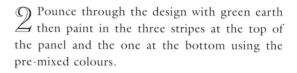

3 Use the no. 10 brush to paint in the man's body. If you find that you produce very noticeable brushstrokes and feel that they are visually distracting, soften them with the goat's hair brush. Fill in the whole shape first with Herculaneum earth, then darken it in places with red earth. Use the original as a guide to the distribution of the colours. Use the no. 0 brush and red earth darkened with burnt umber to paint in the details of the hands, ear and eyebrow. Use black for the iris of the eye and titanium white mixed with red earth and burnt umber for the white. Yellow ochre and burnt umber are used for the necklace, and the lips are painted in titanium white mixed with red earth.

4 With the no. 10 brush and the prepared blue, paint in the 'hat' and the blue on the fish. Vary the tone by diluting the colour in places.

5 Use the no. 10 brush and the prepared yellow ochre to paint in the fish bellies. Use a more dilute colour in places, in order to introduce some variation in tone. Paint in the details on the fish in black using the no. 0 brush. Use the no. 10 brush to paint the fisherman's hair in black.

6 Paint in the fish gills with the no. 0 brush and titanium white, 'dirtied' with some burnt umber. With the same brush, paint the ropes with yellow ochre and add detail to them in black. Soak the sea sponge in water then squeeze it out. Take up a little dilute burnt umber on the sponge and use it to darken the fisherman's body in places. Delicately sponge red earth and burnt umber onto the background in places, to simulate the distressed qualities of the original.

SGRAFFITO BIRD

The word 'sgraffito' comes from the Italian *graffiare* to scratch. Incised lines are perhaps the oldest form of artistic expression, and scratching or cutting into a plaster surface is an ideal way to use this graphic technique for wall decoration.

The Victorian artist, Heywood Sumner, was a famous exponent of sgraffito decoration. He executed a number of large schemes in the technique, notably the decoration of St Agatha's Church in Portsmouth. Sumner applied plaster in a range of different colours to make a base coat then, having applied a thin plain top coat, cut through it to reveal the colours beneath. In an article in the 'Studio' magazine of April 1898 he summed up the special qualities particular to sgraffito: 'The inner surface of the actual wall changes colour in a puzzling but orderly sequence as the upper surface passes into expressive lines and spaces, delivers its simple message and then relapses into silence...the marks of the float, trowel and scraper remain, and combine to make a natural surface'.

This bird design is based on a detail of one of Heywood Sumner's sgraffito murals. A deeper layer of top-coat plaster than his has been used in order to create a more dramatic play of light and shade. The edges of the cut line have been rounded to complement the fluid lines of the design.

MATERIALS

Approx. 1kg (2lb 3oz) base-coat plaster mix

◆

Paint kettle

◆

Trowel

◆

Plant spray or decorator's brush

◆

30 x 30cm (1ft x 1ft) terracotta tile

◆

Approx. 725g (1lb 9oz) top-coat plaster mix

◆

Nail

◆

Palette knife

PIGMENTS

Approx. 8 tbsp ultramarine pigment to tint the plaster

Ultramarine pigment is mixed with the plaster to create a coloured base coat.

1 Combine the ultramarine pigment with the base-coat plaster mix, adding the pigment a little at a time and mixing well until you have an even colour throughout. If the mix becomes too stiff, about a tablespoon of water can be added in this case. (Too wet a mix will be prone to crack.) If the plaster is still too hard, add more lime putty. It is important to find out at this stage what the dry colour will look like. To test, flatten a small lump of plaster and dry it somewhere warm. If the colour is too light, add more pigment. If the colour is too dark, add more plaster. When happy with the colour, apply the plaster and allow it to dry completely.

2 Dampen the tile with the plant spray or decorator's brush until it has absorbed as much water as it can comfortably hold. Plaster with the top-coat mix.

3 Allow the plaster to dry until it is quite firm, but still damp and cool to the touch. Transfer the design to the surface by tracing over the pattern with the nail. You should use enough pressure to leave a slight indentation on the surface. (Soon after you begin, lift up a corner of the design to check whether the impression is clear enough.)

4 Use the palette knife to cut through the plaster. The lines of the design are 'V'-shaped grooves created by using the knife to cut at an angle. Start with the sea, cutting out each side of the lines before lifting out the plaster with the point of the knife. Round the edges of the grooves with the palette knife.

5 Cut out the bird using the same technique as for the sea. The fine lines on the tail and wings are left as shallow grooves in the top-coat plaster. On this scale these details would be too heavy and interrupt the flow of the design if they were cut as deeply as the main outline.

BORDER OF LEMONS

G arlands of fruit and flowers are familiar decorative motifs. This vibrant border, inspired by the strong Mediterranean colours of Italy's Amalfi coast, is a contemporary variation on a traditional theme.

MATERIALS

30 x 90cm (1ft x 3ft) board coated with EML and approx. 3.1kg (7lb) base-coat plaster mix and 2.1kg (4½lb) top-coat plaster mix

♦

Pounce bag or soft mop brush

♦

Palette

♦

Mahlstick

♦

Brushes: 2.5cm (1in) flat soft hair, no. 10 soft hair pointed, 2.5cm (1in) fan-shaped softener

By repeating the design, the border has been used to frame a doorway, contrasting with the plain walls and giving the room a welcoming feeling of sunshine and energy. The pattern could also be used as a frieze. Instead of fixing panels to the wall, you may wish to consider applying plaster directly to the wall on a hessian support using the technique described on page 116.

The blue used in the painting is cobalt blue light, a vivid yet airy colour which is close to the 'Egyptian blue' used by the Romans and Greeks. If your supplier does not stock it, cerulean or ordinary cobalt blue are good substitutes, but remember to keep the colour strong and alive by using it in its pure form, not mixed with white.

PIGMENTS

Pre-mixed

Background wash and blue stripes: *1½ tsp cobalt blue light*

Light green on leaves and green stripes: *1 tsp yellow ochre, ⅛ tsp chromium oxide combined*

Dark green on leaves: *¼ tsp cobalt blue light, ½ tsp viridian combined*

Stem: *½ tsp Herculaneum earth*

Lemons: *1 tsp yellow ochre, ¼ tsp titanium white combined*

On the palette *a little burnt umber and burnt sienna; ½ tsp titanium white and yellow ochre*

Pigment for pouncing the design
½ tsp green earth

1 When the plaster is the right consistency for painting, pounce on the design. Place about a third of the cobalt blue light on the palette and dilute it into a thin wash. Use the 2.5cm (1in) flat brush and the no. 10 brush to apply this wash around the leaf and branch shapes. The brushstrokes should show – they give the design more life and movement – but do use the softening brush to blur any marks that contrast too much with the adjacent areas. Paint in the blue stripes along the edges of the panel.

2 Use the no. 10 brush to paint on the light green stripes and the light green sides of the leaves. Use the same brush to paint in the dark green areas.

3 Paint in the stem in a wash of Herculaneum earth. If the blue has overlapped the stem and is difficult to cover up, darken the wash with more Herculaneum earth then add a little titanium white to make it more opaque. Paint in the lemons, adding the shadows in yellow ochre.

4 Use the no. 10 brush to deepen the shadow on the underside of the lemons with Herculaneum earth mixed with yellow ochre. Use burnt umber mixed with Herculaneum earth to add shadow to the underside of the branches. Paint in the veins on the leaves with yellow ochre mixed with titanium white. Use viridian to define the dark edges of the leaves. Darken the tips of the leaves with viridian and give them fine, curling points. Touch in any missing areas of blue around the stem, leaves and lemons. Finally, use titanium white to give the sunny side of the lemons a highlight and a few white speckles to imitate the pitted texture of citrus skin. A mahlstick will help steady your hand.

BIRD ON A VASE

From the House of the Orchard, Pompeii

S ome of the loveliest Roman frescoes are those from Pompeii. Birds and architectural details are given life with quick, light brushstrokes. It is by enlivening the carefully drawn shapes with these airy, spontaneous strokes, that the spirit of this style of painting can best be recreated. This detail is from a frieze that runs around the upper part of the walls of a small room in the House of the Orchard, in Pompeii. The paintings, which are still on the walls of the house where they were found, feature beautifully observed birds perched on vases and swooping through the air, among masks and architectural ornaments, beneath hanging garlands of leaves.

MATERIALS

*30 x 30cm (1ft x 1ft)
terracotta tile covered with
approx. 725g (1lb 9oz)
top-coat plaster mix*

◆

Nail

◆

Palette

◆

Sea sponge

◆

*Brushes: no. 10 soft hair
pointed, no. 4 soft hair
pointed, no. 3 soft hair pointed*

*When the finished
fresco had dried,
it was rubbed
back in places to
distress the
surface.*

34

PIGMENTS

Pre-mixed
Sky: *1 tsp cerulean, 1½ tsp titanium white, 1 tsp green earth combined*
Vase and ledge: *½ tsp titanium white, a little green earth and burnt sienna combined; ½ tsp green earth*
Bird: *½ tsp cerulean, ½ tsp black combined; ¼ tsp burnt sienna, a little black combined*

On the palette *a little yellow ochre, burnt sienna, titanium white and black*

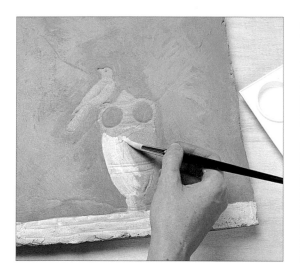 

1 When the plaster is the right consistency for painting, score through the design following the method given on page 14. Use the no. 10 brush to paint the sky around the vase and above the ledge. Dilute the colour in places to introduce variations in tone. Use the no. 10 brush to paint the ledge and the body of the vase and the no. 4 brush for the neck and handles.

2 With a small sea sponge dab a little darker colour – made by adding some yellow ochre and burnt sienna to the original vase mix – on the vase and ledge. Use the no. 3 brush to paint lines of green earth on the vase. Vary the tone of the line in places by diluting the mix. Try to make decisive brushstrokes: don't worry if they don't follow the design exactly.

3 Use the no. 4 brush to paint the body of the bird. Use the no. 3 brush for the beak and feet, using a mixture of burnt sienna and black. With the same brush, highlight the feathers and eyes with titanium white.

4 To create an 'aged' feel to the painting similar to that of the original, use the no. 3 brush to paint a few white lines to imitate repaired cracks in the surface. Outline these with a fine grey line made from titanium white mixed with a little black.

37

ETRUSCAN DOLPHINS

From the House of the Lionesses, Tarquinia

MATERIALS

30 x 90cm (1ft x 3ft) board coated with EML and approx. 3.1kg (7lb) base-coat plaster mix and 2.1kg (4½lb) top-coat plaster mix

♦

Palette

♦

Pounce bag or soft mop brush

♦

Mahlstick

♦

1.5m (5ft) parcel string

♦

Clean, dry pot

♦

Brushes: 2.5cm (1in) flat soft hair, goat's hair softener, no. 4 rigger (or soft hair pointed brush of a similar size), 2cm (¾in) flat soft hair, no. 10 soft hair pointed, 2.5cm (1in) fan-shaped softener, no. 4 soft hair pointed

This copy of a famous image, dating from 520 BC, is from one of the Etruscan sites at Tarquinia in central Italy. It is made up of beautiful strong colours and forms which, though painted as flat patterns, have a great sense of movement and spontaneity. Closer observation revealed that some of the shapes in the repeat pattern had been left out; whether this was deliberate or a mistake made when working in haste is not known (I favour the latter explanation!). In my interpretation I chose to complete the pattern. The straight lines at the top of the waves and the bottom of the pattern would have been used as a guide for laying out the design. These lines would have been 'snapped' in with a piece of string coated with pigment which was, in the case of many Etruscan paintings, fixed by the plaster. Impressions of the string itself have been found in Minoan and Roman paintings, and in places the impressions left by the hands that held the string can also be seen. This method of setting out a design on the wall is still used today and it is used in step 6 of this project. You may wish to practise the snapping technique on a piece of paper or test panel first: mistakes cannot easily be corrected!

This tiny, framed detail was painted onto a thin layer of plaster spread onto the back of a standard bathroom tile.

The final piece has been 'aged' when dry by rubbing it back with fine sandpaper in places.

PIGMENTS

Pre-mixed

Outlines and light brown areas:
  3 tsp Herculaneum earth

Waves: ¼ tsp black, ¼ tsp raw umber, ½ tsp
  ultramarine, ¼ tsp titanium white combined

Green shapes: 2 tsp viridian, 1 tsp cobalt blue
  light, ½ tsp titanium white combined

Blue shapes: 1 tsp cobalt blue light, ½ tsp
  ultramarine, ½ tsp viridian, ¼ tsp titanium
  white combined

Dark brown shapes: 2 tsp burnt umber, 1 tsp black
  combined

On the palette 1 tsp titanium white, ½ tsp raw
sienna, ½ tsp raw umber, ½ tsp burnt umber, a
little black and a little cobalt blue light

Pigment for pouncing the design
1 tsp Herculaneum earth

1 When the plaster is ready to paint, make up some very dilute washes of titanium white tinted with a little raw sienna and white tinted with a little burnt umber. Use the 2.5cm (1in) brush to paint some patches of colour randomly onto the plaster surface, in imitation of the variations in colour of the original. Remember that the plaster is going to be a much lighter colour when it is dry, so do not worry if the colours hardly show at this stage.

2 Use the large goat's hair softener to blur the marks almost immediately, before it sinks into the plaster.

3 Allow any water transferred to the plaster surface whilst painting the washes to be absorbed, then pounce through the whole of the design with Herculaneum earth pigment.

4 When the tracing paper has been removed, the pounced design will be revealed on the surface of the plaster.

5 Paint in all the outlines using Herculaneum earth and the no. 4 rigger. You will probably find that a damp brush pulled through the pounced pigment will be sufficient to outline the design, but if necessary thin down a little of the prepared Herculaneum earth mixture on the palette and use this as well. You may find it helpful to support your hand with the mahlstick as you guide the brush around these fairly complex outlines.

6 'Snap' in the straight lines across the top of the waves and the bottom of the pattern. Coil up a piece of string and put it into a pot of Herculaneum earth pigment. Shake the pot so that the string is coated with powder. Take the string out and carefully remove excess pigment from it by running your thumb and forefinger along its length. The string should be held about 5mm (¼in) above the surface, aligned with the pounced line and pulled taut (you will need to ask a helpful bystander to hold one end for you). When the string is in position, use your thumb and forefinger to grasp it firmly at a point roughly at the centre of the line to be snapped. Pull the string upwards about 13mm (½in) then release it. The string will make contact briefly with the surface, depositing a neat line of pigment.

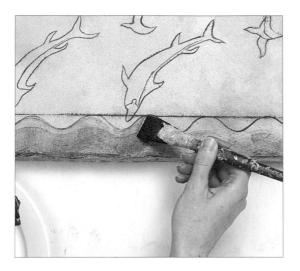

7 Use the 2cm (¾in) brush to paint in the waves with the prepared colour. Following the curves with the brush will produce a swirling pattern and give life and movement to the sea. Dilute the colour in places to introduce variation in the tone.

8 With the no. 10 brush, paint in the green shapes with the prepared mixture. Dilute it in places and in others 'dirty' it with a little of the pigment on the palette so as to introduce subtle variations of tone and colour. With the small fan brush, blur the brushstrokes here and there. It is not necessary to follow all the outlines exactly; a little irregularity helps to recreate the fresh, spontaneous feel of the original.

9 With the no. 10 brush, paint in the blue shapes in the same way as the green areas.

10 Paint in the two tones of brown in a similar way to the blue and green shapes, but introduce a little more variation in colour and tone. Use the no. 4 brush to fill in the details.

This lively scene comes from the House of Hunting and Fishing in Tarquinia.

WATERCOLOUR LANDSCAPE

MATERIALS

*30 x 30cm (1ft x 1ft)
terracotta tile covered with
approx. 725g (1lb 9oz)
top-coat plaster mix*

◆

Large palette

◆

Paper towel

◆

Needle

◆

*Brushes: no. 24 squirrel hair
(or an alternative suitable for
creating very soft washes),
goat's hair softener,
no. 10 soft hair pointed,
no. 0 soft hair pointed*

A small box of watercolours is so easily portable that I make a habit of having my paintbox, pad and pencil with me most of the time. I have searched for a medium that can capture the softness and spontaneity of watercolour and yet can be used in mural decoration. Experiments with oil and acrylic were unsatisfactory: the colours sometimes seemed muddy and lost their strength when stretched out in thin washes or glazes, and a pencil line interpreted as a painted line lost some of its crispness. As soon as I started to interpret watercolour with fresco, I knew that I had come up with an idea that could be developed into an interesting fresco technique. The design is given as an example; you may wish to work from a painting or photograph of your own.

PIGMENTS

On the palette
*a little ultramarine, cerulean, cobalt blue light, titanium white, caput mortum,
red earth, chromium oxide, green earth, yellow ochre, burnt umber and black*

1 When the plaster is ready to paint, paint in the sky with the no. 24 brush, softening the brushstrokes as you go. Use very dilute washes of ultramarine, cerulean, cobalt blue light, titanium white, caput mortum and red earth. Use a paper towel to blot off any excess water between washes. Encourage the colours to blend and flow at first (feel free to spatter and splash the paint onto the surface), then build up more solid colour to define the cloud shapes. (If necessary, use the no. 10 brush for details.)

2 Paint in the main areas of the landscape with the same method, using chromium oxide, green earth, yellow ochre, cerulean, burnt umber, black and caput mortum.

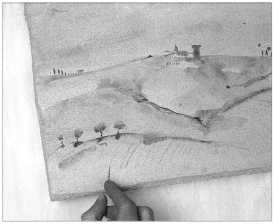

3 Using the full range of colours and the no. 10 brush, paint in the trees and buildings and define the edges of the hills. You may wish to use a no. 0 brush for details such as the tree trunks.

4 Use a needle to score lines imitating the pencil lines found in watercolour paintings. Use the pointed end for fine lines and the 'eye' end for stronger marks. You may wish to emphasise the perspective by using stronger marks in the foreground.

Another sketch of the same landscape, translated into fresco.

LIMEWASH HERBS

MATERIALS

1.5m (5ft) parcel string

◆

2 clean, dry pots

◆

Disposable palette (once dried, limewash is quite difficult to remove)

◆

Masking tape

◆

Pounce bag or soft mop brush

◆

Plant spray

◆

Brushes: no. 0 soft hair pointed, no. 10 soft hair pointed

Limewash has been used to decorate the interior and exterior of lime-plastered buildings for thousands of years. As well as being an interesting decorative technique in its own right, it can be used to add detail to frescoes that have dried, a technique sometimes called *fresco secco* from the Italian *secco*, meaning dry. Paintings executed in limewash adhere best to fairly fresh lime plaster and the ideal surface has a key to it, made in this case by floating the top-coat plaster before it dried. The surface should be dampened down before painting.

All the colours should be tested before you start painting as they do become dramatically lighter when dry. Painting a little out on paper is a good testing method: the colours will dry quickly, which is useful if you find that you need to try a few mixes before getting the precise colour you want. Limewash should be used with care. It is a runny paint that can splash, and the caustic lime can injure both eyes and skin. Goggles and gloves are, therefore, sensible precautions when painting large areas.

This design is suitable for a kitchen, and can be adapted by using different plants or text. Most word processors have an interesting range of fonts that can be enlarged and used for pounced designs if you do not feel confident in your sign-writing skills.

For this pattern, simple bold brushstrokes work best. You may prefer to practise a few different leaf patterns on paper first, before deciding exactly what to paint. Remember that with limewash, which does not depend on damp plaster to fix the colours, there is no urgency about the speed at which you paint; you can come back to it whenever you want, though do bear in mind that once the paint is on it is difficult to remove. If your walls are not lime plastered, this design would work equally well painted on a panel coated with base-coat plaster mix.

PIGMENTS

Limewash colours, in separate pots with lids, each prepared from 2 heaped tsp sieved lime putty, mixed well with about 70ml (2½ fl oz) water (use lime water if available). The paint should be the consistency of milk. Into each pot add about 1 level tsp of the following: black, bright green, yellow ochre, chromium oxide, Herculaneum earth, caput mortum and viridian. One pot should contain the white limewash mix, without any additional colour.

Pigment for pouncing the design *½ tsp titanium white, ½ tsp black*

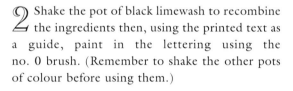

1 Snap in white guide lines marking the position of the top of the text and base of the plant stems using the method described on page 41. Draw a straight line on the pounce across the top of the lettering and align this with the snap line. Tape the words to the wall, adjusting the spacing until you are satisfied with the result. Pounce through the words with a little black pigment.

2 Shake the pot of black limewash to recombine the ingredients then, using the printed text as a guide, paint in the lettering using the no. 0 brush. (Remember to shake the other pots of colour before using them.)

3 Mix a little of the bright green, yellow ochre and chromium oxide on the palette. Paint in the sprig of basil with the no. 10 brush, using the design as a guide. With the no. 0 brush, add the characteristic light veins with white to which a little of the green has been added.

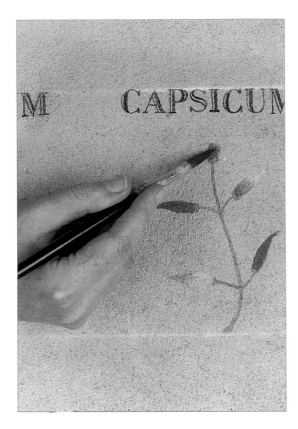

4 Paint in the branch of peppers, using the no. 10 brush. Each pepper is at a different stage of ripening. Use Herculaneum earth for the red peppers and caput mortum for the purple areas. The yellow is yellow ochre. The green pepper at the bottom right, is painted with the basil leaf green at its base, to which a little white and yellow ochre has been added before painting the tip. The stem is chromium oxide.

5 Paint the chives with the no. 0 brush. The stems are painted in a mixture of greens. Chromium oxide is mixed with a little yellow ochre for the light leaves. The dark leaves are painted in chromium oxide mixed with viridian. The chive flowers are stippled on in caput mortum and caput mortum mixed with white, over which flecks of pure white are added.

6 Paint in the rosemary with the no. 0 brush. The stem is painted in caput mortum and the leaves in viridian mixed with chromium oxide.

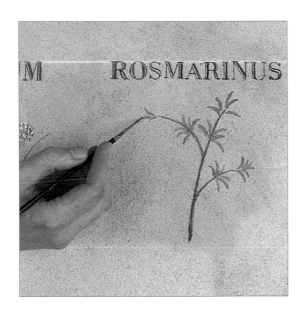

OLIVE BRANCH NICHE

From the House of the Golden Bracelet, Pompeii

S imple olive branch designs are found in both Roman and Etruscan decoration. This particular scheme is taken from a fresco painting found in a niche built into a wall at Pompeii. Frescoes outdoors need to have their edges protected from the rain, because moisture getting in between the layers of plaster causes deterioration, particularly in cold weather. Traditionally, frescoes are protected either by an overhanging roof or a stucco border. Today pollution poses an additional threat to exterior frescoes, though many decorative schemes that have been well maintained have survived on the outside of buildings for hundreds of years.

To plaster an outdoor niche, prepare it according to the instructions on pages 124-5. If you wish to decorate a plaster niche indoors, line it with hessian as described on page 118. You will find an old spoon useful for smoothing the curves.

Work such as this, painted within a niche, is reasonably well protected from the elements. If it is eventually affected by damp or frost, the natural 'distressed' quality brought about by this deterioration can be very attractive in its own right.

MATERIALS

30 x 60cm (1ft x 2ft) niche lined with approx. 3.75kg (8lb 5oz) top-coat plaster applied over rough and base coats as necessary

◆

Palette

◆

Brushes: no. 10 soft hair pointed, round long bristled hog hair brush (sometimes called a fresco brush), or a round soft hair brush, with a ferrule width of about 13mm (½in)

These swallows and lilies are taken from a Minoan fresco that dates from between 1550 and 1500 BC.

PIGMENTS

Pre-mixed
Green leaves: *2 tsp green earth, ½ tsp titanium white combined; 1 tsp green earth, 1 tsp cobalt blue light, ½ tsp titanium white combined*
Brown leaves: *1 tsp raw sienna, ½ tsp titanium white combined; 1 tsp raw sienna, ¼ tsp titanium white combined*

On the palette *½ tsp chromium oxide, ½ tsp caput mortum, ¼ tsp black*

1 Sketch in the stems with the no. 10 brush and the lighter green mix. Use the larger brush to paint in the green leaves, using both of the green mixes, then darken some of the leaves with chromium oxide.

2 Paint in the brown leaves with the two mixed colours, using the same brush as you used for the green leaves.

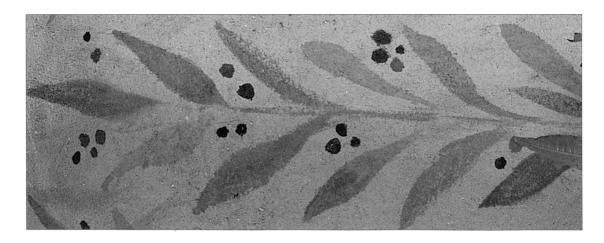

$\mathcal{3}$ Add the olives using the caput mortum pigment and the no. 10 brush. Darken some of the olives by mixing black into the caput mortum. Diluting the colours with water creates lighter olives.

PEACH AND VASE

From the Archaeological Museum, Naples

MATERIALS

*30 x 30cm (1ft x 1ft)
terracotta tile covered with
approx. 725g (1lb 9oz)
top-coat plaster mix*

♦

Pounce bag or soft mop brush

♦

Palette

♦

Mahlstick

♦

*Brushes: 2.5cm (1in) flat soft
hair, goat's hair softener,
no. 4 soft hair pointed,
1cm (½in) flat soft hair*

This composition was inspired by one of a series of Roman still lifes from Pompeii and Herculaneum. My simplified version omits some of the branches of fruit, but includes the glass vessel and green peaches from the original.

The still lifes of this period were very accurately observed, with great attention being paid to effects of light and the contrast in texture and colour between objects. The compositions were often arranged on shelves, as in this case. The vase is not particularly believable as a form, but the deft way in which its highlights and shadows have been painted gives such a vivid impression of light and reflection that the imperfections of the perspective become quite irrelevant. You may find it helpful to have a glass vessel available for reference when painting.

The different styles of Roman painting are known by numbers. This still life is in the fourth style, which was current at the time of Pompeii's destruction in August, AD 79.

PIGMENTS

Pre-mixed
Dark stripes: ½ tsp caput mortum, ½ tsp black,
¼ tsp burnt sienna combined
Medium stripe: 1 tsp Herculaneum earth,
½ tsp burnt sienna combined
Light stripe: ½ tsp titanium white, 1 tsp burnt
sienna combined
Dark green: 1 tsp viridian, ½ tsp chromium oxide
combined
Light green: ½ tsp titanium white, 1 tsp chromium
oxide, 1 tsp yellow ochre combined

On the palette 1 tsp titanium white, ½ tsp yellow
ochre, ½ tsp burnt sienna, ¼ tsp caput mortum,
½ tsp black, ¼ tsp viridian, ½ tsp burnt umber

Pigments for pouncing the design ½ tsp burnt
sienna, ½ tsp green earth, ½ tsp titanium white

1 When the plaster is the right consistency for painting, pounce on the design. Use burnt sienna to pounce through the horizontal divisions of the shelves then use the 2.5cm (1in) brush and the pre-prepared colours to paint in the four stripes. Soften some of the brushstrokes with the goat's hair brush. To introduce variations in the colour and tone of the stripes, dilute the colours in some places and add a little of one of the earth tones or the white from the palette in others.

2 Pounce through the peach and vase design. Use green earth for the branch and peaches and white for the vase. Use the no. 4 brush dipped in water and the pigment deposited on the surface during the pouncing, to paint in the outlines. Take care to wash away any heavy deposits of pigment left on the outline of the vase. It is important to ensure that the guide line is sketched in as softly as possible because you will need to create a lot of contrast between it and the bright white highlights later on.

3 Mix together some of the light and dark greens and use the 1cm (⅜in) brush to paint in the leaves, stem and outer part of the peach. You may wish to use a mahlstick to support your hand when painting these shapes.

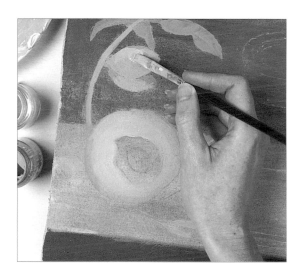

4 Start to use the light green to add highlights to the stem and fruit, blending the tones with the goat's hair brush. At this stage you can also begin to blend in a little of the darker green in places, as you start to establish the forms.

5 Continue to build up the volume of the fruit, using the 1cm (⅜in) brush to add more contrasting highlights. Add more white and yellow ochre to the light green mix if necessary.

6 Use the no. 4 brush to add more detail to the fruit and stem. Use the dark green mix for the shadows and a little white mixed with yellow ochre and 'dirtied' with a little dark green for the highlights.

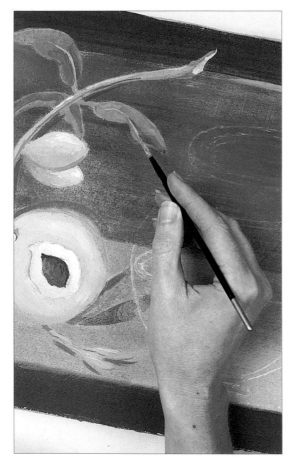

7 Use the no. 4 brush to paint in the flesh around the kernel, using titanium white mixed with yellow ochre. Highlight the top edge with white. Paint in the kernel with burnt sienna mixed with caput mortum. Paint in the pits on the kernel with caput mortum mixed with black. With the same brush darken the leaves in places with a little viridian mixed with burnt umber. Paint the veins on the leaves in light green plus a little white. Fine shadow lines on the stem can be added in burnt umber mixed with a touch of the light green mix.

Paint on the shadows below the leaves, stems and vase: use the mid-tone shelf colour mixed with the dark tone shelf colour for shadows on the mid-tone areas and the mid-tone mixed with the light tone for the shadows on the light areas. The shadow beneath the vase is darker than the shadows under the fruit and leaves (a little burnt umber was added to the dark shadow mix). Remember to leave a lighter area within the vase's shadow. The leaf which can be seen through the vase is also painted at this stage. Take care to introduce a break where it passes behind the glass. The area seen through the water is painted in lighter tones than the other leaves, and softened and blended well.

8 Use the no. 4 brush to paint in the shadows on the vase. Make the grey tone by mixing a little of the light green mix into titanium white and black. Vary the tone in places, using the photograph as a guide.

9 Use the no. 4 brush to paint in the highlights with titanium white. Prepare a dilute mix, only adding more pigment to it for the brighter areas. Work from dark to light, putting on the brilliant highlights last. For the larger highlights that form the band of light running down the vase, make sure that the paint is very dry and 'scuff' it across the surface, working horizontally. The highlights are painted in two stages: use the more dilute mix first then add a few tiny spots of bright white.

ABSTRACT PANEL

In this piece the border is made up of plain plaster, into which flakes of natural mica have been mixed. When I first experimented with this effect, I had not heard of other examples of its use. I have since discovered that various natural stones have been added to plaster mixes at different times throughout history to create delicate, sparkling surfaces. The glitter pigment cannot readily be painted over as it isolates the pigment from the carbonising effect of the lime plaster. It would, in any case, lose its sparkle when painted over. Glitter pigments can be mixed with coloured plaster, though the plain plaster colour is, perhaps, the most elegant. Like the other colours, glitter pigments should be tested for lime fastness before use.

This project was inspired by eastern imagery, so the patterns for the moulds have an oriental feel. The use of both raised modelling and stamped impressions is traditional to fresco. The Minoans created raised relief figures. In the Renaissance, saints' halos were often both raised and stamped with decorative motifs.

One of the pigments used in this project is cinabrese. If this is not available, you can make a similar colour by combining 4 parts burnt sienna with 1 part titanium white. Alternatively, you may wish to choose an entirely different colour scheme.

MATERIALS

Approx. 5 x 5cm (2 x 2in) piece
air-drying modelling clay

♦

Needle or small nail

♦

Acrylic varnish

♦

Approx. 5.5kg (12lb) top-coat plaster mix

♦

Trowel

♦

Bucket or paint kettle

♦

75 x 90cm (2ft 6in x 3ft) board coated
with EML and approx. 8kg (17lb)
base-coat plaster mix

♦

Plant spray or decorator's brush

♦

Palette knife

♦

Palette with separate wells

♦

Fine and medium grade sandpaper

♦

Dust mask

♦

Brushes: soft hair mop, 4cm (1½in) flat
soft hair, goat's hair softener

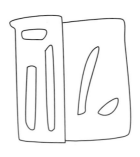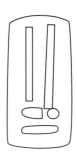

PIGMENTS

Approx. 9 level tbsp white or neutral-coloured mica to tint the plaster

On the palette *½ tsp burnt sienna, ½ tsp yellow ochre, ¼ tsp Herculaneum earth, ¼ tsp burnt umber, 1½ tsp cinabrese, ¼ tsp graphite flakes*

Limewash colours, in separate pots with lids, each prepared from 2 heaped tsp sieved lime putty, mixed well with about 70ml (2½ fl oz) water (use lime water if available). The paint should be the consistency of milk. Make up a pot each of yellow ochre and venetian red by adding 1 level tsp of pigment to the basic recipe.

1 To make a mould, form a rectangle of modelling clay and use a needle or nail to score the lines into it. Allow the mould to dry then seal it with a couple of coats of acrylic varnish. Test the print by pressing it into a patch of spare plaster. (You will get the clearest impression when the plaster has become quite firm.) Make as many moulds as you wish, using the same method.

2 Mix the mica and 2.5kg (5lb 8oz) of plaster together in the paint kettle, stirring until the mica is distributed evenly. Prepare the board by using a plant spray or decorator's brush to dampen the base-coat plaster thoroughly.

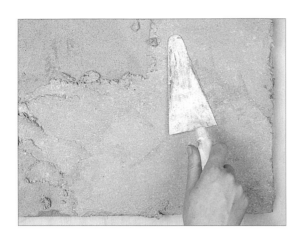

3 Use a trowel to apply the plaster to the outside of the board. Spread the plaster up to about 5cm (2in) beyond where the cut edge of the central section will be. (Use the photograph of the finished piece as a guide.) At this stage, leave the edge of the plaster ragged.

4 When the plaster has become reasonably firm, press the moulds into the surface. If the impressions are not clear enough, smooth the plaster over, allow it to dry for a little longer then re-apply the moulds.

5 Use the soft hair mop brush to dust some more glitter pigment over the surface of the damp plaster and carefully press it down with the trowel, taking care not to disturb the plaster.

6 Use a palette knife or the point of the trowel to cut back the edge of the completed section. Give the piece a bevelled edge, sloping away from the finished area. Leave to dry.

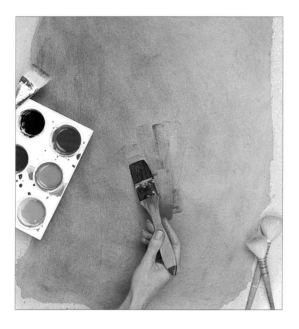

7 Dampen the base-coat plaster of the remaining area, including the edge of the completed section, then plaster it with the remaining top-coat mix. In this case, rather than making the traditional flat join between the two *giornate* (see page 78), allow the plaster in the centre to overlap the outside section by a fraction to create an irregular, delicate edge. When the plaster is ready to paint, dilute the pigments on the palette into thin washes. Apply the colours with the 4cm (1½in) brush, softening the brushstrokes where necessary, using the finished piece as a guide.

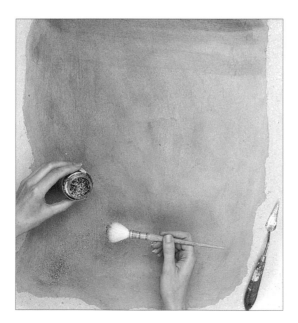

8 Paint in two stripes with burnt sienna and yellow ochre then apply the graphite by sprinkling it onto the surface and gently pressing it in with the palette knife. Continue to add colours and marks until you are satisfied with the result then allow the piece to dry.

9 When the panel has dried (this may take about a week), 'distress' the surface by sanding back areas and scratching into the surface with the nail (wear a dust mask when sanding). Look at photographs of the soft, worn colours found on the outside of Mediterranean houses and other old, battered painted surfaces, and incorporate these into your design.

10 Paint on the limewash. As limewash keeps almost indefinitely, I have a number of mixed colours at the studio which are left over from other projects. I happened to have some of the right colours stored in these large jars, but you should use the smaller quantities listed under Pigments.

MEDITERRANEAN LANDSCAPE

MATERIALS

30 x 45cm (1ft x 1¼ft) board coated
with EML and approx. 1:65kg
(3lb 8oz) base-coat plaster mix and
1.1kg (2½lb) top-coat plaster mix

♦

Pounce bag or soft mop brush

♦

Palette

♦

Mahlstick

♦

Brushes: 2.5cm (1in) flat soft hair,
goat's hair softener, no. 10 soft hair
pointed, no. 0 soft hair pointed

This view of Capri, beyond a balustrade, is painted in bright blues and earth colours. The sea and sky are brushed on in washes that allow the reflective plaster to glow through, thus making use of the luminous qualities particular to fresco painting. If you wish to create particularly brilliant colours in fresco, adding marble dust, or the coarser marble meal, to the top-coat plaster mix can produce a very bright ground. Using about 1 part sand to 2 parts marble dust will create a very light coloured plaster that will give added luminosity to the colours.

The steps show branches of figs at the top of the panel, but you could substitute lemons based on those painted in the 'Border of lemons' project if you prefer.

PIGMENTS

Pre-mixed
Sky and sea: ½ tsp cerulean, ½ tsp
  cobalt blue light, ½ tsp green earth
Tablecloth, balustrade, boats and
doves: 1 tsp titanium white
Figs: ¼ tsp caput mortum, ½ tsp
  titanium white combined
Leaves: ¼ tsp viridian, ½ tsp yellow ochre,
  a little titanium white combined

On the palette a little ultramarine,
Herculaneum earth, burnt sienna,
caput mortum, viridian and
yellow ochre

Pigments for pouncing the design
½ tsp green earth, ½ tsp titanium white

1 When the plaster is ready to paint, pounce in the horizontal lines in green earth. Dilute the two sky and sea blues on the palette. Use the 2.5cm (1in) brush to apply the paint, softening the brushstrokes as you go. Build up a cerulean area at the top of the sky. Use more cobalt blue light for the central area. Use very dilute washes where the sky meets the sea. The sea is cobalt blue light on the horizon, cerulean in the central area and cerulean overlaid with green earth mixed with a little titanium white in the foreground. Paint in the tablecloth with titanium white.

2 Pounce in the cloud, doves, island, boats, waves and tablecloth with titanium white pigment. Using the no. 10 brush, darken the cloud with cobalt blue light mixed with a little ultramarine and titanium white. Use the no. 0 brush and a mixture of titanium white and cerulean to paint in the boats, adding shadows beneath them in dilute ultramarine. (Use the same mixture to paint in the doves.) The waves in the foreground are painted in cerulean, ultramarine and titanium white. Mix ultramarine with a little titanium white for the checks on the tablecloth and use it undiluted where two stripes cross. Either use the no. 0 brush to paint on the stripes freehand, or use a ruler as a guide as explained on page 97. The stripes are softened in places to make them more subtle. Paint in the island with the no. 10 and the no. 0 brushes. Wash on dilute mixes of Herculaneum earth and burnt sienna. Introduce some soft lilac, using titanium white mixed with caput mortum.

3 Pounce in the foliage and balustrade with titanium white. Use the no. 10 brush and the prepared titanium white to paint in the balustrade. Add a shadow line around it with ultramarine mixed with some of the white. You might find it helpful to use a mahlstick to steady your hand when painting the details.

4 Paint in the branches, leaves and figs. Use the no. 0 brush and Herculaneum earth mixed with titanium white for the branches and the no. 10 brush and the prepared colours for the leaves and figs.

5 Use the no. 0 brush to add highlights and shadows to the fig tree. For the shadows on the leaves, darken the green with viridian and ultramarine; lighten it with white and yellow ochre to add highlights. Use pure caput mortum for the dark shadows on the figs. Add white to the fig colour for the highlights. The shadows on the branches are painted in burnt sienna. A few ultramarine lines are added around the branches. Continue to refine the details until you are satisfied with the result.

GEOMETRIC RELIEF

MATERIALS

30 x 30cm (1ft x 1ft) terracotta tile covered with approx. 1kg (2lb 4oz) base-coat mix

◆

Approx. 725g (1lb 9oz) top-coat plaster mix

◆

Plant spray or decorator's brush

◆

Trowel

◆

Palette

◆

Nail

◆

Palette knife

◆

Ruler

◆

Brushes: 2.5cm (1in) flat soft hair, goat's hair softener

In fresco, a design can be scratched or cut into the surface of the plaster. A nail or needle can be used to scratch roughly into the surface; more precise designs can be cut out with a palette knife. Sometimes the under or top coat of plaster is painted in one or more colours. The shadows cast by the cut edges of the plaster emphasise the pleasing relief effect which is an integral part of the design as was seen in 'Sgraffito Bird' on page 26.

This design was inspired by Mediaeval tiles in the British Museum. It would work well on a larger scale, but could only be used indoors as the small shapes with their exposed edges would be too vulnerable to frost and damp to be exposed to the elements. To ensure a good bond between the two layers of plaster, the base coat should be roughened well with a float before the top coat is applied. The addition of pigment to the mix makes it more prone to cracking so dry the piece very slowly, by wrapping it in plastic.

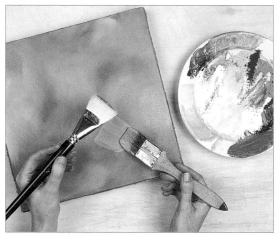

1 Combine the top-coat plaster with the burnt sienna pigment and test the colour by following the method given on page 28. Dampen the tile with a plant spray or decorator's brush until it has absorbed as much water as it can comfortably hold, then plaster immediately with the coloured mix.

2 When the plaster is ready to paint, mix up dilute washes of all the pigments listed and use the 2.5cm (1in) brush to paint them onto the surface in patches. Blur the marks with the goat's hair softener straight away. Build up the colours, making them stronger and more opaque in areas, using the photograph as a guide. Allow the plaster to dry until it is quite firm but still damp and cool to the touch, then transfer the design to the surface by tracing over the pattern with the nail as described on page 14.

3 When the tracing is complete, cut away the unwanted areas of plaster. First cut around a shape, using the palette knife to make a slanting, bevelled edge that slopes away from the shape that is to remain.

4 Use the palette knife to lift out the unwanted plaster. Keep the point of the palette knife flat so as not to dig into the base-coat plaster.

5 You may wish to use a straight edge as a guide for cutting long straight lines. A ruler with a bevel, placed bevel side down, works best. It allows you to see a little way under the edge of the ruler, enabling you to control the blade better. When you have cut away all the plaster, hold the panel upright and use a soft brush to remove any remaining fragments. If any crumbs remain on the base-coat areas, use the palette knife to scrape them away.

INLAID STILL LIFE

This colourful piece is painted in limewash colours on a variety of different coloured plaster sections. The quantity of plaster prepared is more than you will use in the project; there will be enough left over to keep as wet samples of colour, should you wish to have them for reference. Store the plaster mixes in tightly sealed paint kettles until you are ready to use them. As the pigment-saturated plaster tends to be rather dry, you can protect it further from evaporation by giving the surface a light spray of water and pressing a plastic bag down over it before sealing the container.

The limewash can be applied when the plaster is just ready to paint or, preferably, when it is completely dry. In this example, most of the paint was applied the day after the plaster had been laid. Paint can be added at any stage, but be sure to dampen the surface first.

MATERIALS

Approx. 1kg (2lb 3oz) top-coat plaster mix

◆

Approx. 350g (9oz) top-coat plaster mix combined with 4 tbsp lime-proof bright green, 1 tbsp titanium white, 1 tbsp cobalt blue light

◆

Approx. 350g (9oz) top-coat plaster mix combined with 4 tbsp burnt sienna, 2 tbsp raw sienna

◆

Approx. 350g (9oz) top-coat plaster mix combined with 4 tbsp ultramarine

◆

Approx. 350g (9oz) top-coat plaster mix combined with 3 tbsp caput mortum, 1 tbsp ultramarine, 3 tbsp titanium white

Paint kettles with lids

◆

Trowel

◆

90 x 90cm (1½ft x 1½ft) board coated with EML and approx. 1.5kg (3lb 5oz) base-coat plaster mix

◆

Plant spray or decorator's brush

◆

Pounce bag or soft mop brush

◆

Palette

◆

Needle or nail

◆

Brushes: 2cm (¾in) flat soft hair, no. 10 soft hair pointed

PIGMENTS

Limewash colours, in separate pots with lids, each prepared from 2 heaped tsp of sieved lime putty, mixed well with about 70ml (2½ fl oz) water (use lime water if available). The paint should be the consistency of milk. Into each pot add about 1 level tsp of the following: titanium white, cerulean blue, cobalt blue dark, venetian red, yellow ochre, caput mortum, viridian, lime-proof bright green, Herculaneum earth and black.

Pigment for pouncing the design
½ tsp titanium white

1 Test the coloured plaster using the method given on page 28. Prepare the board by dampening the base-coat plaster then pounce on the outlines of the different plaster areas. Begin with the vase shape, plastering about 2.5cm (1in) further than the cut line will be. Re-pounce the outline of the vase and, when the plaster is firm, use the palette knife to cut away the excess, making a bevelled edge that slopes away from the outline. A second *giornata* can added almost as soon as the first is firm, but it is best to wait until the following day. This is because the base coat as well as the cut edge of the previous day's section need to be dampened down before the new area is plastered. If too much water is applied to a very fresh plaster edge, it may start to soften and dissolve. To line the fresh edge up with the dry one, plaster as usual, but when you are very close to the cut edge of the previous day's *giornata*, press the trowel downwards, forcing the plaster across and up to the dry edge. Fill in the dip you have made by pressing the trowel down, and finish in the usual way. Any traces of plaster that have got onto a painted area should be removed immediately. The lime in the fresh plaster will stain the painted layer.

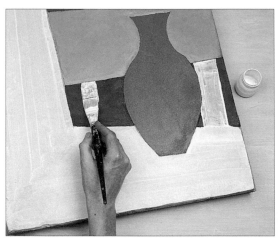

2 Cover all the plain plaster with titanium white using the 2cm (¾in) brush, then paint the white stripes on top of the section of blue plaster.

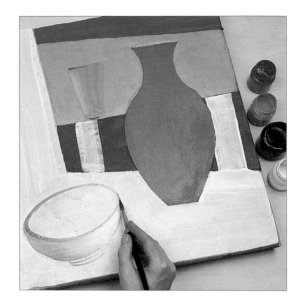

3 Paint the blue vase that is on the shelf in cerulean with a cobalt shadow line. Pounce in the shape of the bowl, then paint it in with a mixture of black and titanium white, using the no. 10 brush. Add the shadow on the curtain with a diluted version of the same colour.

4 Use the caput mortum to paint in the figs, adding detail to them with caput mortum to which a little titanium white has been added.

5 Paint the green fig in the foreground and the leaves in the blue vase with bright green. Deepen the base of the fig with viridian and add yellow ochre to its tip. Paint the pattern on the fabric with dilute yellow ochre and dilute bright green to which a little viridian has been added. Add a little caput mortum to the shadows on the curtain. The pear is painted in yellow ochre with a shadow line in Herculaneum earth.

6 Allow the plaster to dry slowly under plastic. When completely dry, score fine lines onto the figs to imitate the patterns on their skin. Dampen the plaster and work back over any areas you wish to refine, painting shadows beneath the big vase, bowl and fruit, and adding further details until you are satisfied with the result.

THE PROCESSION OF THE MAGI

From the east wall of the Chapel of the Magi, Palazzo Medici Ricardi, Florence

Benozzo Gozzoli painted the fresco cycle of the Procession of the Magi during the second half of 1459. Gozzoli used a mixture of very well-executed fresco and tempera techniques which, combined with the careful way in which the chapel was built, means that these are amongst the best preserved Renaissance fresco cycles.

Originally the chapel had very little natural light and the frescoes were designed to be seen by candlelight. The semi-darkness would have accentuated the visual impact and three-dimensional quality of the panting. The lavish gold decoration would have looked magnificent glowing in the soft flickering light. The extensive use of gold, silver and ultramarine, the most expensive decorating materials, were an expression of the wealth of the Medici family, a message that would have been understood by all the visitors they received in the Chapel.

The procession of the three kings – Caspar, Balthazar and Melchior – with their attendants, is painted on three walls of the Chapel. Melchior, on the west wall, represents sunset and old age. His red robe and the reds in the background are autumnal colours. Balthazar, representing maturity, is painted on the south wall, dressed in green, the colour of summer.

The detail used for the project comes from the east wall. Caspar, the young king, is dressed in white, symbolising dawn and spring. The whole of the procession appears to start from the white castle, above the figure of the king, and to wind down through the section of landscape chosen for this project.

In order to mix colours close to the ones that Benozzo Gozzoli would have used, lime putty is used in the lighter colours except in the case of highlights.

PIGMENTS

Pre-mixed

Grass: *1 tsp green earth, ¼ tsp yellow ochre combined*

Brown trees:

Background and light tone: *¼ tsp yellow ochre, ¼ tsp raw sienna, ½ tsp lime putty combined*

Medium tone: *½ tsp burnt sienna, ½ tsp yellow ochre combined*

Dark tone: *¼ tsp black, ¼ tsp burnt umber, ¼ tsp lime putty combined*

Highlights: *¼ tsp titanium white, ¼ tsp yellow ochre combined*

Blue trees:

Medium tone: *2 tsp lime putty, ½ tsp ultramarine, ¼ tsp black combined*

Dark tone: *½ tsp lime putty, ½ tsp ultramarine, ¼ tsp black, ¼ tsp raw umber combined*

Light tone: *2 tsp lime putty, ¼ tsp ultramarine, ¼ tsp black combined*

Green trees and hedges:

Medium tone: *½ tsp yellow ochre, ¼ tsp viridian, ¼ tsp chromium oxide, ¼ tsp green earth, ¼ tsp lime putty combined*

Dark tone: *¼ tsp chromium oxide, ¼ tsp ultramarine, ¼ tsp black, ¼ tsp raw umber, ¼ tsp lime putty combined*

Light tone: *½ tsp yellow ochre, ½ tsp lime putty combined*

On the palette *¼ tsp yellow ochre, ½ tsp lime putty, ¼ tsp green earth, ¼ raw umber, ¼ tsp titanium white, ¼ tsp viridian, ¼ tsp chromium oxide, ¼ tsp raw sienna, ¼ tsp black*

Pigment for pouncing the design

½ tsp green earth

1 When the plaster is the right consistency for painting, pounce on the design. Use the 2cm (¾in) brush to paint in the grass. Vary the colour by adding a little more green earth to the colour in places and a little yellow ochre and lime putty in others. Use the fan-shaped brush to blend the colour if necessary.

2 Paint a dilute wash of the light brown colour over the trees with the 2cm (¾in) brush.

3 Divide the hair of the no. 20 brush into four separate points. Wrap the string around the handle a few times then use it to divide the hair in two across its centre. Turn the string around the handle a few more times then divide the brush again, at right angles to the first division, to create four separate points. Wrap the remaining string tightly around the handle, tying the ends together securely and cutting off the excess. This customised brush is a traditional tool for painting leaves. If you prefer, a small piece of natural sponge can be used instead. Use the brush or sponge to stipple on the main horizontal bands of the tree, using undiluted light brown.

4 Add the medium brown in the same way.

5 Paint in the dark brown with the same method. Use the no. 4 brush and the darkest colour to create separate clumps of foliage. Add highlights to the leaves with the lighter brown. (You may find referring to your pounced design useful when building up the shape of the trees.) Note that the brown tree in the foreground is lighter than those in the middle distance.

6 Paint in the hedging and blue and green trees in the same way. Work back over all the trees once you have blocked them in, adding more detail until you are satisfied with the overall composition.

7 Paint the brown tree trunk with the medium brown colour with green earth added to it for the shadow. The trunk of the green tree is painted in green earth mixed with raw umber and lime putty, with titanium white added for the highlight. This tree has a few almost white highlights and some green leaves which are painted in a mixture of the medium tone green and viridian. Paint the grass, adding details with the no. 4 brush. Use the original green colour, deepened with chromium oxide and green earth for the shadows, and lightened with yellow ochre and titanium white for the other details. A little raw sienna is also added to the mix in places.

8 Paint in the path and rocks in the foreground using the 13mm (½in) brush and dilute lime putty. Add grey shadows to the rocks in the foreground by adding a little green earth and black to the lime putty.

9 Use the no. 0 brush to paint in the top of the palm tree, visible in the foreground. The light stripes are painted in a mixture of yellow ochre and lime putty. The dark stripes are painted in chromium oxide, yellow ochre, lime putty and a little viridian.

10 Use the no. 0 brush to paint in the figure (you may wish to use the mahlstick to support your hand). The man's jacket is painted with the light and medium browns, his trousers, boots and hat, with a mixture of black, lime putty and the medium brown mixture.

CUPID AND URN

From the House of the Vettii, Pompeii

The paintings of cupids from the House of the Vettii are some of the best-known images in Roman painting. The scenes of tiny figures earnestly engaged in various trade activities are painted on a black background, with a vermillion band below and large vermillion panels above. In my design, some elements from the decorative scheme of the rest of the house have also been included. The border around the central black panel is made up of two very narrow columns, connected by curling plant tendrils. The candelabra shapes on each side of the cupid are typical 'grotesque' forms. When Roman paintings were rediscovered in Renaissance times they were often underground. The Italian word for caves is *grotte*, hence the name given to this style of painting. The painting of grotesques was revived by Italian artists of the early sixteenth century, most notably Raphael who used the grotesque style to decorate the famous *loggie* in the Vatican.

Egg tempera is used to paint the cupid and details on the central black panel. You should be aware, before you start to paint, that egg tempera paint dries almost immediately. Any marks you wish to rethink should be removed, by washing with water on a paint brush, fairly quickly.

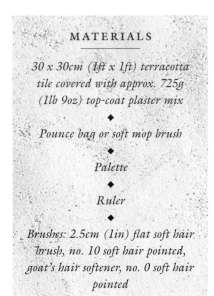

MATERIALS

30 x 30cm (1ft x 1ft) terracotta tile covered with approx. 725g (1lb 9oz) top-coat plaster mix

◆

Pounce bag or soft mop brush

◆

Palette

◆

Ruler

◆

Brushes: 2.5cm (1in) flat soft hair brush, no. 10 soft hair pointed, goat's hair softener, no. 0 soft hair pointed

PIGMENTS

Pre-mixed
Borders: *1 tsp Herculaneum earth,*
   1 tsp green earth, 1 tsp black, 1½ tsp raw umber,
   ½ tsp yellow ochre

On the palette *titanium white*

Pigment for pouncing the design
½ tsp green earth

1 When the plaster is the right consistency for painting, pounce on the design using green earth. Paint in the borders with the 2.5cm (1in) brush and the no. 10 brush. Use Herculaneum earth for the outside, green earth for the middle stripe, and black for the central area. Use raw umber for the area between the plant tendrils and the green earth border. Leave some of the plaster showing as a guide for the position of the columns, base line connecting the columns and the plant tendrils.

2 Use the no. 10 brush to paint in the yellow ochre border, columns and tendrils. Add highlights in titanium white and shadows in Herculaneum earth. Use the design as a guide but bear in mind that improvising with spontaneous marks will produce a painting more in keeping with the original than trying to make an exact copy of it. Leave the panel to dry thoroughly, which may take about a week.

EGG TEMPERA

Materials *1 egg, needle, 2 bowls, a little
distilled water (or tap or cooled boiled water)*

◆

Pigments on the palette *a little yellow ochre, raw sienna, titanium white, green earth and black,
Herculaneum earth*

◆

Pigment for pouncing the design *½ tsp titanium white*

 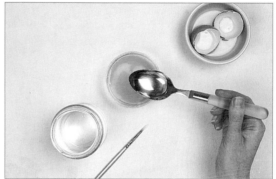

3 When the panel has dried, prepare the egg tempera. Carefully break open a fresh egg and separate the yolk from the white by passing the egg from one half shell to the other. When you have removed as much of the white as you can, tip the yolk into the palm of your hand and pass it gently from one hand to the other until all of the white has been removed. Pierce the egg sack with a needle and allow the yolk to run out into a clean container. Discard the egg sack (if the yolk breaks during the separation process, or bits of the egg sack fall into the separated yolk, sieve the mixture as well as you can).

4 Add water to the yolk, using about the same volume as that of the yolk itself. (This mixture will be diluted further for washes, etc., so there is no need to be absolutely accurate at this stage.) Combine the water and egg together thoroughly by stirring well with a brush or shaking in a sealed jar. Wash all brushes, surfaces and your hands really well after handling raw egg.

5 Pounce on the design lightly in white. Make up a palette of tempera colours. Take up a little egg mixture on the no. 0 brush, transfer it to the palette and mix in some yellow ochre pigment. Dilute this further with water and paint in the candelabra and vine branch. Add a little white for the highlights. Use yellow ochre for further variations in tone. Paint in the vine leaves with a mixture of yellow ochre, green earth and white, using yellow ochre mixed with white for the highlights and green earth for the shadows.

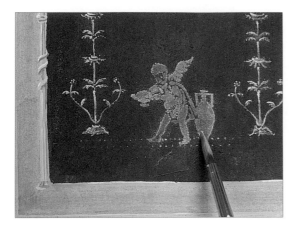

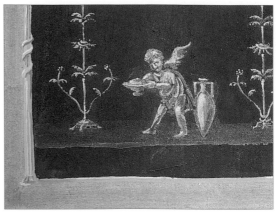

6 Use the no. 10 brush to block in the cherub and amphora with a yellow ochre wash.

7 Paint in the lighter tones on the cherub and amphora using the no. 10 brush and a wash of white mixed with yellow ochre. Leave some of the black showing through in the areas where the darkest tones will be. Wash in the 'shelf' with the same colour, using a more opaque mix in the foreground and an almost transparent wash in the background.

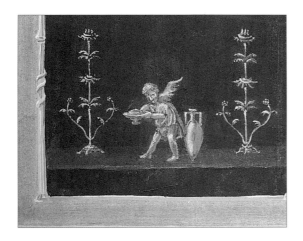

8 With the no. 10 brush, use a wash of raw sienna combined with a little yellow ochre to establish some mid-tone areas on the figure and amphora, giving the piece a bit more strength and colour.

9 Using the no. 0 brush and the range of colours on the palette, continue to refine the image. Use black to obliterate any dried marks you wish to rethink. Remember that the original cherubs were painted quite quickly and, in some cases, roughly. If your image becomes too detailed it may lose some of the quality of the original. Finally, add a stripe of Herculaneum earth below the shelf using the method for painting straight lines described on page 97.

*On this small tile, vermillion has been washed over the Herculaneum earth border
using egg tempera as a binder.*

BUTTERFLY AT A WINDOW

I n this project, plain and coloured plaster mixes are blended together to produce a marble effect, using a technique which is similar to that used to make *scagliola*, an imitation stone made from plaster of Paris.

MATERIALS

Approx. 2.1kg (4 ½lb) top-coat plaster mix, of which 1.1kg (2½lb) is reserved for the upper part of the panel

♦

2 paint kettles

♦

Trowel

♦

60 x 45cm (2ft x 18in) board coated with EML and approx. 3.5kg (8lb) base-coat plaster mix

♦

Plant spray or decorator's brush

♦

Palette knife

♦

Palette

♦

Pounce bag or goat hair mop

♦

Ruler, about 10cm (4in) wider than the panel

♦

2 supports of equal height

♦

Brushes: 5mm (¼in) and 13mm (½in) soft hair lining fitches (or 13mm (½in) filbert soft hair); 4cm (1 ½in) flat soft hair, goat's hair softener, no. 0 soft hair pointed, 2.5cm (1in) fan-shaped softener, no. 10 soft hair pointed

Fresco has been used to create a variety of stone effects since ancient times. The Romans painted elaborate imitation onyx and marble onto lime plaster. In Renaissance Italy, trompe l'oeil stone panels were sometimes painted below the fresco cycles on the walls. The cool plaster surface of this 'stone' was often waxed and buffed to a soft sheen to heighten the illusion of real marble.

Painted stone was used for practical reasons other than economy. Where a wall was not strong enough to support marble cladding, paint was used instead. Sometimes, more dramatic colours and patterns than those found in natural stone were required to complement the rest of a decorative scheme.

In this project, two different plasters are mixed together in imitation of a grey marble. The pattern is enhanced, after the plaster has dried, with the

addition of details in egg tempera. The panel is divided into two *giornate*. In this case, the marble is painted first but if you want to paint the piece on a wall the upper section should be completed before the lower one, to ensure that no fresh plaster falls onto a painted area.

PIGMENTS

Approx. 5 tbsp black pigment to tint the plaster

Pre-mixed
Dark lines: *½ tsp black, a little titanium white combined*
Medium tone lines: *½ tsp titanium white, ¼ tsp black combined*
Light lines: *½ tsp titanium white*
Sky: *½ tsp cerulean, ½ tsp titanium white, ½ tsp cobalt blue light, ½ tsp cinabrese*

On the palette *¼ tsp titanium white, ¼ tsp Herculaneum earth, ¼ tsp cobalt blue light, ¼ tsp black*

Pigment for pouncing the design
½ tsp titanium white

1 Place 425g (15oz) plaster in a paint kettle and combine it with the black pigment. If the mix becomes too stiff, about a tablespoon of water can be added. If the plaster is still too hard, add more lime putty. It is important to find out at this stage what the dry colour will look like. To test, flatten a small lump of plaster and dry it somewhere warm. If the dry colour is too light, add more pigment. If it is too dark, add more plaster. Keep this sample – you will test the paint tones on it in step 3.

As this sample shows, the plaster dries much lighter than the wet plaster mix might lead you to expect.

2 Using the template as a guide, make a mark on each side of the panel at the point where the marble will end. Thoroughly dampen the base coat within this area with a plant spray or decorator's brush. Use the trowel to apply alternating blobs of plain and black plaster over the area. At this stage, the plaster should extend about 2.5cm (1in) beyond the marks. Smooth the plaster with the palette knife to create a diagonal pattern. Allow the plaster to firm up a little.

3 Pounce on the line that defines the edge of the marble. Cut away the excess, using the palette knife to create a bevelled edge that slopes away from the finished section. (You may wish to use the ruler as a guide, as explained on page 75.) Test the colours on the dry piece of plaster and adjust the tones if necessary. Paint the dark lines first, using the small lining fitch. Place the ruler bevel side up on two supports (mixing pots, for example). The ruler should be slightly below and parallel to the line you wish to paint. Hold the brush so that the bristles are flat on the surface, and the handle is pressed firmly against the ruler. Pull the brush very lightly across the surface. Be careful not to disturb the wet plaster. If necessary, apply two coats of colour to build up the required tone. If you are using a soft filbert brush rather than a lining fitch, hold it side on for the fine lines and turn it so that the bristles are at a right angle to the ruler when you paint the wide mid-tone bands.

4 Use the larger fitch to paint in the medium bands. You will need to make two strokes, one above the other. Blur the marks with the fan softening brush as you go.

5 Use the small fitch to paint on the light bands. Leave the plaster to dry thoroughly; this might take about a week.

 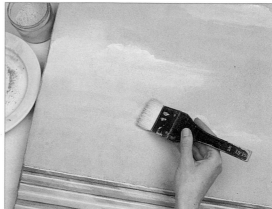

6 Dampen the base-coat plaster and the cut edge of the 'marble' and plaster the sky area. When the plaster is ready to paint, use the 4cm (1½in) brush to wash on patches of cerulean, white and cobalt blue light, diluted on the palette. Blur the brushstrokes with the goat's hair softener. Either use the finished project as a guide or seek inspiration from painted skies by artists such as Tiepolo.

7 Paint on the cinabrese clouds using the same brush and softening the strokes almost immediately. The pale pink won't show up well at this stage. Painting in light tones on the dark, wet plaster requires practice. If your first attempt doesn't have enough contrast when dry or if, on the other hand, the colours appear too raucous, they can be adjusted with tempera.

EGG TEMPERA

Materials *1 egg, needle, 2 bowls, a little distilled water (or tap or cooled boiled water)*

◆

Pigments on the palette *½ tsp chromium, ½ tsp green earth, ½ tsp burnt umber, a little titanium white, Herculaneum earth, cobalt blue light, black*

◆

Pigment for pouncing *½ tsp black*

8 Prepare egg tempera using the method given on page 91. Paint in the trees using the no. 10 brush. Dab on varied mixtures of the tree colours to build up the form.

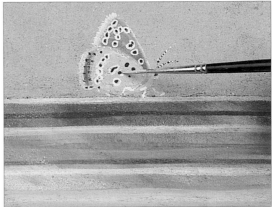

9 Pounce on the butterfly with titanium white. Block in the colour of the wings using the no. 0 brush and titanium white mixed on the palette with Herculaneum earth and titanium white mixed with cobalt blue light.

10 Use the same brush to add detail to the butterfly. Paint the spots in black and outline them with white. Use the same colours for the antennae and legs. The body is painted in the blue wing mix, to which a little black has been added. Leave to dry for a week.

11 Paint in the veins on the marble with a no. 0 brush and black and grey tempera. In this case, a book of photographs from a marble supplier provided inspiration for the pattern on the marble, but were not copied slavishly.

99

VATICAN MAP

From the Gallery of the Maps, the Vatican

This project is based on a detail from the Gallery of the Maps which was decorated between 1580 and 1583 by Ignazio Danti, during the pontificate of Gregory XIII. Danti painted the walls of the corridor with frescoes depicting maps of Italy. At the north end of the gallery, Pope Gregory built the 'Tower of the Winds' from where observations were made that led to the replacement of the Julian Calender with the Gregorian Calender that we still use today.

MATERIALS

30 x 30cm (1ft x 1ft) terracotta tile covered with approx. 725g (1lb 9oz) top-coat plaster mix

◆

Pounce bag or soft mop brush

◆

Palette

◆

Mahlstick

◆

Brushes: 2.5cm (1in) flat soft hair, no. 10 soft hair pointed, 2cm (¾in) flat soft hair, goat's hair softener, no. 0 soft hair pointed

Painted maps are visually pleasing as the combination of text, colours and lines of longitude and latitude create harmonious patterns. With an old map there is the added fascination of being taken back through history and seeing the world through the eyes of our predecessors. These maps are particularly stunning because of the wealth of detail: trompe l'oeil city maps are 'pinned' on to the surface of the painting, and illustrations of battles, boats, fish and fantastical gilded scroll work combine with the brilliant blues and greens of the sea and land.

If you wish to create your own maps, the method used to paint this project could be adapted to other designs. Alternative words and numbers can either be handwritten, or traced from fonts available on a word processor.

100

Torre Laconia

MonteSoro

$\mathcal{M}ARE$

GOLFO D

60
41   55

PIGMENTS

Pre-mixed

Trees: *1 tsp green earth; ½ tsp green earth, ½ tsp titanium white combined*

Buildings: *½ tsp Herculaneum earth, ¼ tsp yellow ochre, and a little titanium white combined*

Beach: *½ tsp Herculaneum earth, ½ tsp titanium white, ¼ tsp yellow ochre combined*

Sea: *½ tsp cobalt blue light, ¼ tsp green earth, ¼ tsp titanium white combined*

On the palette: *¼ tsp yellow ochre, ¼ tsp Herculaneum earth, ¼ tsp burnt sienna, ¼ tsp chromium oxide, ¼ tsp ultramarine, ½ tsp titanium white, ¼ tsp green earth, ¼ tsp burnt umber*

Pigment for pouncing the design
½ tsp green earth

1 When the plaster is the right consistency for painting, pounce on the design. Use the 2.5cm (1in) brush to paint in the lighter green of the trees and background. Use the no. 10 brush and the darker green to add shadows. Paint in the beach with the 2cm (¾in) flat brush. The buildings are painted with the no. 10 brush – at this stage paint in the lighter tones. Paint the stripes at the bottom of the map using yellow ochre and Herculaneum earth with the 2cm (¾in) brush. Use the 2.5cm (1in) brush to paint in the sea, then add darker patches to it with the original colour darkened with a little ultramarine from the palette. Blur the darker areas with the goat's hair softener.

2 Paint in the darker tones of the buildings with the no. 10 brush and the original mixture darkened with some burnt sienna. Add details to the trees with the no. 10 and no. 0 brushes. The dark green is deepened further, in places, with a little chromium oxide and ultramarine. Add lighter and darker patches to the beach with the no. 10 brush. The lighter areas are made by adding white to the original mix, the dark areas are deepened with Herculaneum earth. Paint on the general shapes of the waves with a colour made by adding a little white and green earth to the original blue mixture.

3 Use the no. 0 brush to define the tree shapes with dark lines made from the original dark mix, deepened, as in step 2, with chromium oxide and ultramarine. In places, add a little burnt umber to the green to darken it further. Add a little of the sea blue to the landscape and trees with the no. 10 brush. Mix the light green with a touch of yellow ochre and use this to vary the green tones. Paint in the rest of the detail on the buildings with the no. 0 brush, using a combination of burnt sienna and Herculaneum earth. The same brush is used to paint more waves with the original blue mixture, lightened with white. Some of the details are blurred, while others are left crisp. Allow the fresco to dry completely, which may take around a week.

GILDING

Materials *Acrylic or oil size, approx 5 sheets gold transfer leaf, cotton wool ball, squirrel hair mop brush*

◆

Pigment for pouncing the design
½ tsp yellow ochre

EGG TEMPERA

Materials *1 egg, needle, 2 bowls, a little distilled water (or tap or cooled boiled water)*

◆

Pigments on the palette *a little black, burnt umber, burnt sienna.*

◆

Pigment for pouncing the design
½ tsp black

4 Apply a coat of acrylic size to the ochre stripes and allow it to dry for the time indicated in the manufacturer's instructions (it is normally ready to gild when the size has become transparent). Oil-based size may be used as an alternative, but again, follow the manufacturer's instructions. Because the fresco is porous, you will need to apply two coats of size: one to seal it and another to size it.

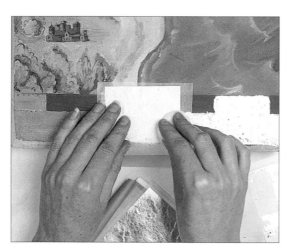

5 Place the gold leaf on the tacky surface (gold side down) then rub the backing paper firmly with a cotton wool ball. This ensures that the gold is pushed into all the irregularities of the plaster surface. (The yellow ochre underpainting on the gold areas means that any tiny fragments of the surface which are not covered with gold will not show up too much.)

6 Each sheet should overlap the preceding one by about 3mm (⅛in). If, when you remove a leaf, any areas are not gilded, simply press more gold onto the surface. If it still fails to stick, you have either left the area unsized, or the size is still too wet. In the former case, apply more size, in the latter, wait a little longer before gilding.

7 Use the squirrel hair mop brush to rub off the loose fragments of gold. At the joins, the brush should follow the direction of the overlap, brushing away from the sheet to which it is attached, not towards it. Rubbing towards the join tends to lift the gold in places, creating a frayed edge and revealing the surface beneath. Pounce on the lettering with yellow ochre. Paint on two coats of size using the no. 0 brush and gild in the same way.

8 Pounce on the outlines of the straight lines, numbers and lettering in black. Prepare some egg tempera following the instructions given on page 91. Paint in the lines using a ruler to guide you. Paint the names of the towns and numbers in black, using the no. 0 brush. Add a shadow line to the gold lettering, using the no. 0 brush and a mixture of burnt umber and burnt sienna. You may find that the egg mixture beads up on the gold. This 'cissing' can be corrected by adding a little more pigment to the mixture. Allow the cissed paint to dry then overpaint it with the stiffer paint mix.

GRISAILLE LUNETTE

MATERIALS

*Semicircular board, radius 48cm (19in),
covered with EML and approx. 3.6kg (8lb)
base-coat plaster mix*

◆

Plant spray or decorator's brush

◆

Approx. 2.45kg (5lb 6oz) top-coat plaster mix

◆

Trowel

◆

Pounce bag or soft hair mop

◆

Nail

◆

Palette knife

◆

Mahlstick

◆

Ruler

◆

2 supports of equal height

◆

*Brushes: 4cm (1½in) flat soft hair, goat's hair
softener, no. 10 soft hair pointed, 1cm (½in) flat
soft hair, no. 4 soft hair pointed, no. 0 soft hair
pointed, 5mm (¼in) soft hair lining fitch, 13mm
(½in) soft hair lining fitch (or substitute 13mm
(½in) soft hair filbert)*

The term grisaille comes from *gris*, the French for grey. As the name implies, it is a painting executed in tones of grey. Grisaille was frequently used in baroque and Renaissance decorative schemes, often with dramatic trompe l'oeil effects of light and shade. In this case, a purple background painted with caput mortum – a rich natural iron oxide pigment traditionally used in fresco – offsets the grey.

This piece, suitable for use as an over-door panel, is based on a detail from within a seventeenth-century decorative scheme.

Because it is to be placed high up on the wall I have painted the shading as if the light source were coming from underneath the piece. If you wish to display the panel in a different position, you may prefer to alter the shading, relating it to the actual light source that will be closest to the piece when it is fixed to the wall. In this way you will make the most of the trompe l'oeil illusions that can be created with the grisaille technique. A piece of plaster ornament can provide a model for sketches of light and shade, which can then be adapted to this design.

PIGMENTS

Pre-mixed

Background: *2 tsp caput mortum,*
  2 tsp titanium white combined
Medium tone: *1 tsp titanium white,*
  1 tsp green earth, ⅔ tsp black combined
Dark grey: *1 tsp black, ½ tsp green earth,*
  a little titanium white combined

Shadow: *1 tsp caput mortum,*
  ½ tsp titanium white combined
Light grey: *1 tsp titanium white,*
  a little green earth combined

On the palette *½ tsp white, ½ tsp black*

Pigment for pouncing *½ tsp titanium white*

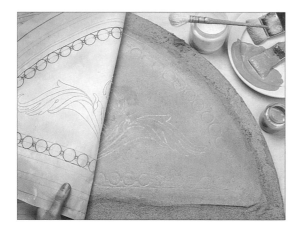

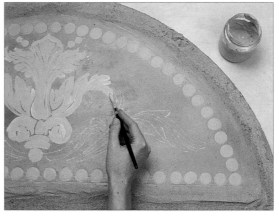

1 Dampen the base coat, then plaster the area defined by the line surrounding the bead border, extending it a couple of inches beyond. Leave the edge of the plaster ragged. When the plaster is ready to paint, apply the background colour with the 4cm (1½in) brush, softening the brushstrokes as you go. Pounce through the central motif. Use a nail to score through the outline of the beads and the line defining the edge of the section to be painted. The beads are scored through as it makes it easier to keep track of their outlines when painting of the different tones.

2 Block in all the shapes with the medium tone grey, using the no. 10 brush. Leave a little of the background colour showing through as a guide for the main lines and tonal divisions within the central motif.

3 Block in the darker tones using the no. 10 and no. 4 brushes, using the finished panel as a guide.

4 Use the no. 10 brush to add the main areas of shadow to the background. Use the same brush and the light grey to block in the highlights on the central motif and bead border. Add some fine lines of crosshatching to the beads with the no. 4 brush, thus blending the light and medium tone greys. Continue to refine and develop the tones, using the finished example as a guide. You may wish to add some pure white highlights at this stage. When you are satisfied with the design, cut back the ragged plaster edge with the palette knife and allow the piece to dry.

5 Use the plant spray or decorator's brush to dampen the base-coat plaster, as well as the cut edge of the finished section. Plaster the remaining area. When it is ready to paint, use the 1cm (⅜in) flat brush to paint in the medium tone areas on the curved top of the panel.

6 Use the 1cm (⅜in) and the no. 4 brushes to paint the light and dark tones. You may find it helpful to use the mahlstick to support your hand at this stage.

7 With the no. 0 brush, and using the finished piece as a guide, paint in some fine dark lines. The dark colour is made by adding some black to the dark tone mix. Add fine titanium white highlight lines in the same way. If you wish, mid tones can be added between some of the dark and light tones, softening the effect. Using the finished piece as a guide, paint in the straight lines at the bottom of the panel. Use either the lining fitches or filbert brush and the method outlined on page 97.

STARS LUNETTE

A sky and star design can be used in many different ways to decorate walls or ceilings. This semicircular piece is ideal as a decorative panel above a door. If your ceilings will not allow this, it would also work if well mounted on the wall. You could distress the surface, and present the panel as an architectural antique. A map of the stars will provide inspiration for other compositions.

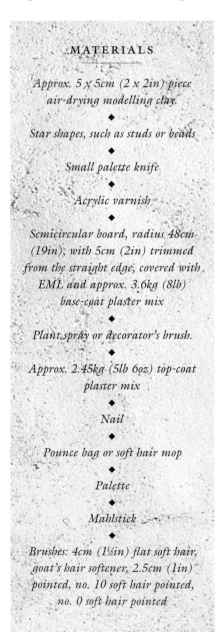

MATERIALS

Approx. 5 x 5cm (2 x 2in) piece air-drying modelling clay.

◆

Star shapes, such as studs or beads

◆

Small palette knife

◆

Acrylic varnish

◆

Semicircular board, radius 48cm (19in), with 5cm (2in) trimmed from the straight edge, covered with EML and approx. 3.6kg (8lb) base-coat plaster mix

◆

Plant spray or decorator's brush.

◆

Approx. 2.45kg (5lb 6oz) top-coat plaster mix

◆

Nail

◆

Pounce bag or soft hair mop

◆

Palette

◆

Mahlstick

◆

Brushes: 4cm (1½in) flat soft hair, goat's hair softener, 2.5cm (1in) pointed, no. 10 soft hair pointed, no. 0 soft hair pointed

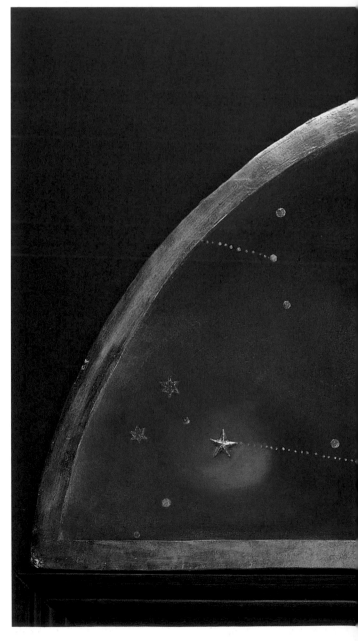

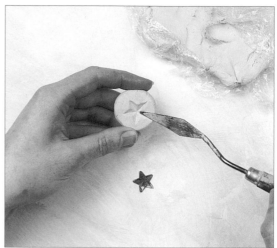

1 Make the moulds for the raised and indented stars. Flatten the base of a piece of modelling clay. If it is very soft and sticky, allow it to dry for a little while until it has a firmer consistency. Press one of the star shapes firmly into the mould.

2 Remove the star and use the point of a palette knife to flatten any irregularities and, if necessary, sharpen up the impression. Allow the mould to dry then give it a couple of coats of varnish to seal it. When the varnish has dried, prepare another piece of clay in the same way.

3 Press the soft clay into the mould you have made so as to create a raised star. You may find that you need to make a few attempts before achieving a clear impression. If necessary, use the palette knife to sharpen up the image as before. Varnish the second mould and allow it to dry.

4 Thoroughly dampen the base-coat plaster, then apply the top coat in the usual way. When the plaster is ready to paint, lay the design on the surface and use a nail to score through the line of the border. Mark the position of the stars to be modelled by pouncing them through.

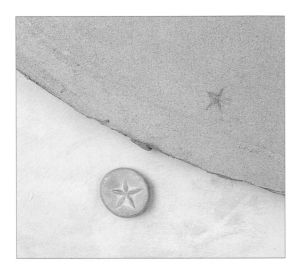

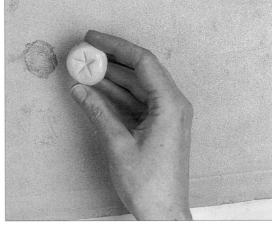

5 To create indented stars, press the raised mould into the plaster. (You may need to sharpen up the points of the stars with the tip of the palette knife.)

6 To make raised stars, apply a small dollop of plaster on the surface of the piece and press the indented mould over it.

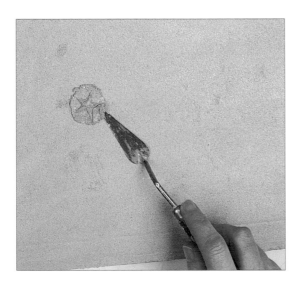

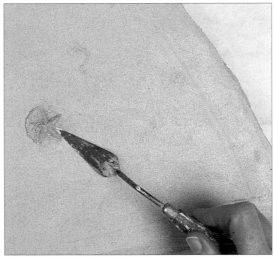

7 Remove the mould then use the tip of the palette knife to cut away the segments between the points of the star.

8 Smooth down the plaster between the points of the stars with the tip of the palette knife.

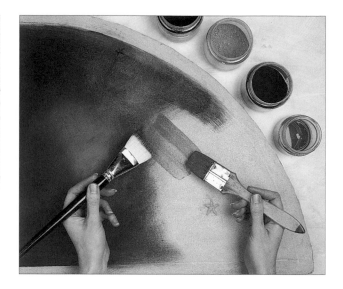

9 Use the 4cm (1½in) brush to paint on patches of the prepared ultramarine and cobalt blue light. Darken the ultramarine with black in places. Dilute the colours with more water in some areas (remember the colours will look lighter when they are dry). Blend the colours together with the goat's hair softener. (Be gentle when painting over the stars.)

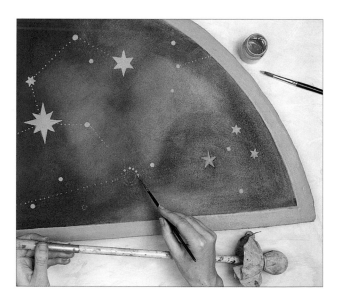

10 Pounce on the constellation in yellow ochre. Use the 2.5cm (1in) brush to paint the border and the no. 10 brush to paint the stars, using the mahlstick to support your hand. Allow the fresco to dry thoroughly; this might take a week.

GILDING

Materials *Acrylic or oil size, approx. 5 sheets gold transfer leaf, cotton wool ball, squirrel hair mop brush*

EGG TEMPERA

Materials *1 egg, needle, 2 bowls, a little distilled water (or tap or cooled boiled water)*

◆

Pigment on the palette *burnt sienna*

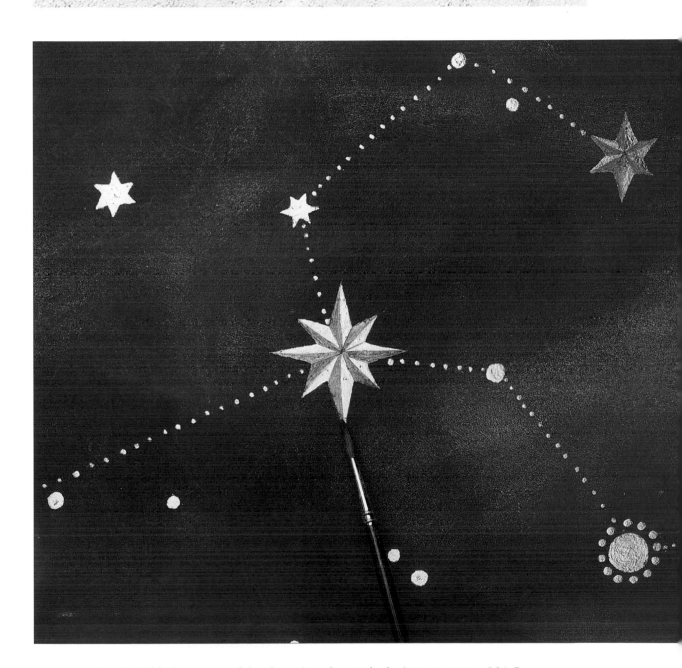

11 Gild the stars and border using the method given on pages 104-5. Then, prepare some egg tempera following the instructions on page 91, and use it to paint burnt sienna onto the stars. Dilute the egg tempera well with water so that when it is brushed on the gold shows through. If the paint beads on the surface, add a little more pigment.

ROMAN FRAGMENTS

From the 'Garden Room' at Livia's Villa at Primaporta, Rome

The best-known and possibly the finest Roman paintings of nature come from the 'Garden Room' at Livia's Villa (now housed in the National Museum in Rome). Painted in around 20 BC, the frescoes decorated a large, partially underground room, which may well have been used as a cool dining area in the summer. Behind a sharply painted little fence and stucco wall are accurately painted trees, flowers and birds. Beyond these, patches of blue and green blur together, creating the feeling of a dense forest. A jagged line of rocks overhangs the sky, giving the impression that the viewer is looking out at the landscape from within a cool grotto.

Something of the charm and airy qualities of these paintings can be brought into a contemporary setting without the need to rebuild a room to accommodate them. The lack of any rigid structure in the design means that individual sections can be copied without losing the overall feeling of the whole. In

MATERIALS

Hessian

◆

PVA glue

◆

Plant spray

◆

Approx. 750g (1lb 10oz) top-coat plaster mix per 30cm sq (1sq ft) of wall

◆

Palette knife

◆

Palette

◆

Brushes: 4cm (1½in) flat soft hair, goat's hair softener, no. 10 soft hair pointed, no. 4 soft hair pointed, no. 20 soft hair pointed (ferrule width about 6mm/¼in)

this project, portions of the fresco are presented as restored fragments. If you wish to recapture the 'distressed' quality of the original, the surface of the plaster can be scratched and sanded when it is dry.

This technique is suitable for walls that are in good condition and sealed with a waterproof coating, such as water-based house paint (the glue will not stick as well to an oil-based paint). Some of the colour mixes for this project are made with titanium white; the Romans would have used lime putty white, which is more translucent. I find that the chalky quality given to the colours with titanium white is useful when imitating Roman fresco, but lime white would certainly be more authentic.

Precise measurements are given for the pigments used in the fragment shown in the steps; for the other fragments, proportions are given for the mix, as the amounts you need will depend on the size of the area you wish to paint.

PIGMENTS

Pre-mixed

Background green, leaves and stems:
½ tsp chromium oxide, ¼ tsp raw umber,
¼ tsp viridian, a little lime putty combined
Daisies: ¼ tsp titanium white, ¼ tsp yellow ochre,
¼ tsp raw sienna

1 Cut a piece of washed and dried hessian into the shape of the fragment you wish to paint. Paint PVA glue onto the wall with an old brush, then apply the hessian. Follow this with another coat of glue, taking care not to go beyond the edge of the fabric. Allow the glue to dry to the point where the hessian is stuck fairly firmly to the wall before plastering.

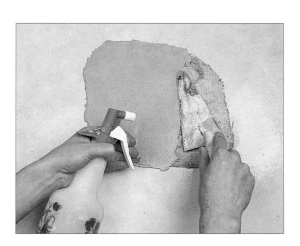

2 Use a plant spray to dampen the hessian before applying the top-coat plaster in the usual way.

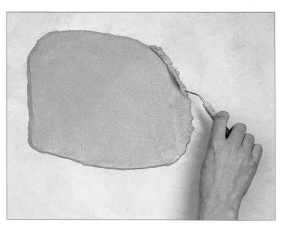

3 Having smoothed the plaster, use the palette knife to cut away the ragged edge, making a neat bevelled edge that slopes away from the plastered area.

4 Paint in the background with a dilute wash of the green, using the 4cm (1½in) brush, blurring the brushstrokes as you go. Use the no. 10 and no. 4 brushes to paint on the leaves with the same colour, using opaque and dilute mixes to vary the tone. Single, spontaneous brushstrokes work best.

5 Use the no. 4 brush to paint in the petals with titanium white and their centres with yellow ochre. If you wish, add a shadow on one side of the centres with raw sienna.

PIGMENTS

Blue sky: *1 part cobalt blue light, ½ part titanium white, ½ part green earth combined*

Leaves and trees: *green earth, chromium oxide, burnt umber, raw umber, yellow ochre, lime putty, titanium white*

Yellow flowers: *1 part yellow ochre, ½ part titanium white combined, with Herculaneum earth shadows and titanium white highlights*

Pomegranates: *1 part Herculaneum earth, ½ part titanium white combined, with Herculaneum earth shadows and titanium white highlights*

Stucco wall: *1 part raw sienna, ½ part titanium white combined for the background. Paint the shadows in burnt sienna and the highlights in titanium white 'dirtied' with a little burnt sienna and yellow ochre.*

Pigment for pouncing *¼ tsp green earth*

The main landscape is painted in the same way as the smaller fragment, but with the help of a large brush, such as a no. 20. First block in the background blue and green tones, overlapping patches of different colours and softening the brushstrokes as you go. Then paint on the trees, flowers and fruit. The straight lines on the wall are painted with a lining fitch and ruler following the method given on page 97, though in this case the ruler is placed directly on the surface of the plaster when it is firm, bevel side up, rather than being held above it with supports.

TIGER

India has a long tradition of fresco painting, but this image of a tiger was inspired by a variety of sources, including frescoes and miniature paintings. The design is painted directly onto a wall. It is divided into two sections only, so the order of painting is simple: the top section first followed by the lower one. This prevents wet plaster falling onto areas that have already been painted. In large schemes it is important to plan the *giornate* at the design stage. They should be simple shapes, falling, as far as possible, at natural visual divisions within the design. In this case, the *giornate* meet along the brow of the hill. Because of the difficulty of matching colours across two *giornate*, large areas of the same colour, such as skies, tend to be painted as single *giornate*. (See Step 1 on page 78 for information of joining *giornate*.)

MURAL WORK

In general, mural work is planned on a scaled-down coloured design (see opposite). Squares are drawn onto this design, then drawn or snapped onto the wall at full scale. In the case of fresco, this takes place when the layer of plaster onto which the top coat will be applied is dry, or at least firm. When all the

squares are drawn out, the design is sketched onto the wall using a mixture of red ochre pigment and water. This outline is known as the 'sinopia', after Sinope, an ancient town on the southern coast of the Black Sea, where the red ochre used for this purpose in Renaissance Italy was found. It is important to see the composition on the wall, full scale, before starting to paint. Any adjustments are made at this stage. When you are satisfied with the design,

Here is my original sketch for the Tiger design. The thick black lines indicate the different sections, or giornate. *The dotted lines are there for squaring up.*

prepare tracings for the different *giornate*. Include the lines of the squares on the tracings: they can be useful as registration marks when you are pouncing the design onto the plaster. For large-scale work, the tracings taken from the sinopia are often transferred to more robust paper (brown parcel paper is ideal), which can stand rougher handling. The designs for the *giornate* are then pricked through, ready for use.

The preparation of the different layers of plaster that are commonly applied as a foundation for a large-scale fresco are outlined in the steps below. For very large projects, artists normally employ a team of professional lime plasterers to lay in the undercoat layers under supervision, only applying the top coat themselves. It is important to be sure that the wall is free from damp. Moisture dissolves salts in the wall which come to the surface and deposit a white powdery substance referred to as efflorescence. As well as being unsightly, efflorescence will cause serious structural damage to the painting.

MATERIALS

<table>
<tr><td>

Stiff brush

◆

Decorator's brush and kettle of water

◆

Plastic sheet

◆

Approx. 27kg (61lb) rough plaster mix, made with 3 parts washed dry coarse sand (max. particle size 3mm/⅛in) and 1 part putty. An optional ½ part goat, llama or cow hair well teased out and in lengths of over 2cm (¾in) can be added to improve the strength of the mix). This will cover an area 1.2m (4ft) square.

◆

Plasterer's 'hawk'

◆

Rubber gloves

◆

Trowel

◆

2 wooden batons 1.2m x 13mm x 8cm (4ft x ½in x 3in)

</td><td>

Masonry nails

◆

Levelling board 1.2m x 13mm x 5-8cm (4ft x ½in x 3in)

◆

Approx. 18kg (40 1/2lb) base-coat plaster mix

◆

Rubber or wooden float

◆

Pounce bag or soft mop brush

◆

Masking tape

◆

Approx. 12kg (27lb) top-coat plaster mix

◆

Palette

◆

Robust ruler or straight edge

◆

Brushes: no. 10 soft hair pointed, 4cm (1 ½in) flat soft hair, goat's hair softener, 2.5cm (1in) flat soft hair, no. 4 soft hair pointed, 13mm (½in) soft hair lining fitch (or 13mm (½in) soft hair filbert)

</td></tr>
</table>

1 Use a stiff brush to remove any loose material from the wall you intend to decorate, then wash away any greasy marks. Ideally the wall should be pointed with lime mortar rather than cement. For important works you may wish to replace cement pointing with lime; take advice from a builder used to working with lime mortar. Thoroughly wet the wall. Allow the water to be absorbed, but be sure that the wall is damp. Lay some clean plastic at the bottom of the wall to catch falling plaster, which can be reused. The plastic also makes cleaning up easier.

2 Mix the rough coat plaster thoroughly. If including animal hair, add it just before you use the plaster and ensure that it is evenly distributed. Apply the rough coat to a depth of about 13mm (½in). Heap a mound of plaster onto a 'hawk' (a square board with a handle beneath it). With a gloved hand, use the trowel to scoop up plaster from the hawk and spread it onto the wall in an upward motion. Lean the hawk against the wall below the area you are plastering so that any plaster that falls off lands back on it. The plaster should be levelled off when you have covered the whole piece, if it is smaller than 1.2m (4ft) wide, or about 1.2m (4ft) square if bigger. To level off, nail a baton each side of the plastered area at right angles to the floor. Pull the levelling board down the wall along these batons. Any plaster over 13mm (½in) deep will be scraped off. Fill in missing areas of plaster then level again. The rough coat should be left with a textured surface, which will act as a key for the next layer.

3 Apply the base-coat plaster to a depth of 1cm (⅜in). It can be added when the rough coat has a firm crust, but is not completely dry. If the rough coat has dried out, wet it well in the same way as you wetted the brick wall. In either case, the rough-coat plaster should be dampened.

4 Apply the base-coat plaster using the same method as for the rough coat. Level it with the float, using a circular motion.

5 Before it dries, scratch a diamond pattern into the base coat with the point of the trowel. On small portable panels, the floated surface is sufficient as a key, but larger areas need the extra support provided by the scratches in the surface. Allow the plaster to dry.

PIGMENTS

Pre-mixed

Sinopia: *1 tsp red ochre, black or other earth colour*

Background: *4 tsp lime-proof bright green, 3 tsp titanium white, 3 tsp cobalt blue light*

Tiger body: *4 tsp titanium white, 2 tsp black*

Border and branch stems: *4 tbsp venetian red*

Pink hill: *½ tsp venetian red, 1 tsp titanium white combined*

Yellow hill and flower: *1 tsp yellow ochre, 1 tsp titanium white combined*

Green line: *½ tsp green earth, ½ tsp chromium oxide combined*

Foliage: *1 tsp green earth, 1 tsp yellow ochre, 1 tsp viridian*

Fine line on border: *2 tsp black*

Pigment for pouncing the design *2 tsp black*

6 Pounce the whole design onto the base coat, using masking tape to support the paper, then use the no. 10 brush to paint in the outline with the sinopia. Make any adjustments at this stage and add them to the pounced design. Divide the design into two parts for the different *giornate*. (If developing your own design, square it up onto the base coat, sketch it in sinopia, then make the tracing for the pounce from the sinopia outline.)

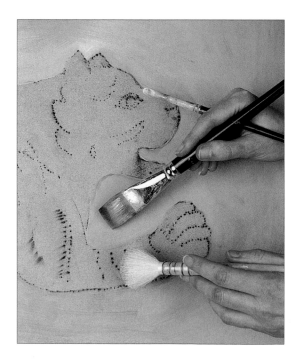

7 Thoroughly dampen the plaster then apply top-coat plaster about 5mm (¼in) deep to an area covering the top *giornata* and extending about 5-7cm (2-3in) beyond its edge. (Leave the edge ragged at this stage.) When the plaster is the right consistency to paint, pounce on the tiger and the line marking the border of the *giornata*. Put some of each of the background colours on a palette and dilute them a little with water. Mix different combinations of these colours and use the 4cm (1½ in) brush to paint them on in overlapping patches around the tiger, softening the brushstrokes as you go. Use the 2.5cm (1in) and no. 10 brushes and the same method to paint the areas around the ears, tail, feet and mouth.

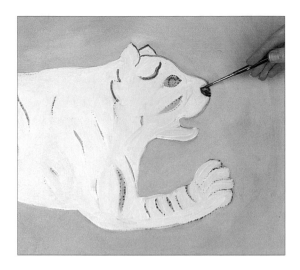

8 Paint in the body of the tiger with titanium white, using the method employed for painting the background. Use the no. 4 and no. 10 brushes to paint in the black stripes and other details. The stripes have a ripple effect created by using a single brushstroke for each stripe and varying the pressure on the brush as it is pulled down the surface. Where there is more pressure a lighter tone is produced. Paint in the top part of the red border with the 4cm (1½in) brush. Paint almost up to the green area then use the lining fitch or filbert brush to paint a straight edge, using the ruler as a guide. Cut away the excess plaster with the point of the trowel or palette knife, creating a bevelled edge that slopes away from the painted area.

9 When the first *giornata* is firm, dampen the the next section to be painted, including the cut edge. Plaster the area with top-coat mix using the method used in Inlaid Still life (see page 78).

10 When the plaster is ready to paint, use the 2.5cm (1in) brush to paint on the pink and yellow hill, blurring the brushstrokes with the goat's hair softener. Paint in the green line defining the top of the hill, varying the tones of the green by adding more water to it in places.

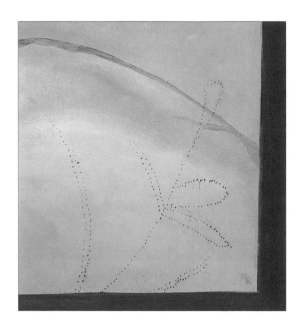

11 Pounce on the plants. Note that in this case the design has been altered a little since the pounce was tried out at the sinopia stage: the top leaf crosses into the first *giornata*.

12 I moved the top leaf down so that it sits entirely within the second *giornata*. This is because it makes more sense to work on the whole branch at once, rather than painting a single leaf in one *giornata* then joining it to those painted on the second section. The tones and mixes within the greens are varied to add interest and a sense of movement to the foliage. Complete the border, using the same method as that used in step 8. Paint in the black line in the same way.

TEMPLATES

The following design templates are taken from the step-by-step projects in this book. Use a photocopier to enlarge the designs to fit the area you plan to paint.

BASILICUM   CAPSICUM   ALLIUM   ROSMARINUS

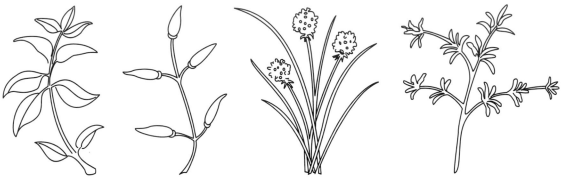

Limewash Herbs, page 48

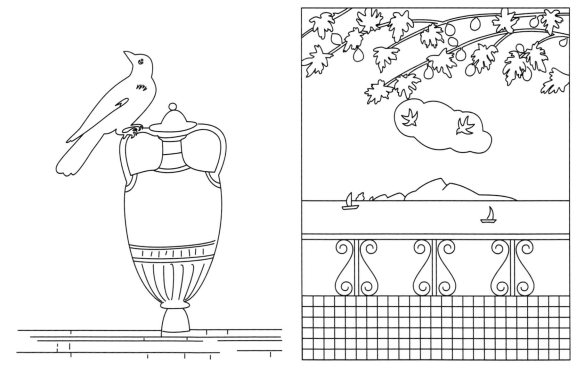

Bird on a Vase, page 34   *Mediterranean Landscape, page 68*

Cupid and Urn, page 88

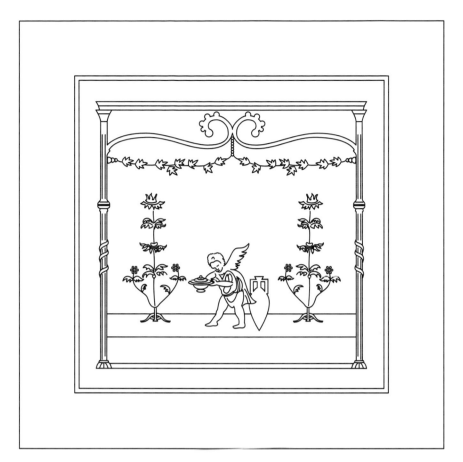

Torre Laconia Monte Soro

GOLFO DI

MARE

Vatican Map, page 100

The Procession of the Magi, page 80

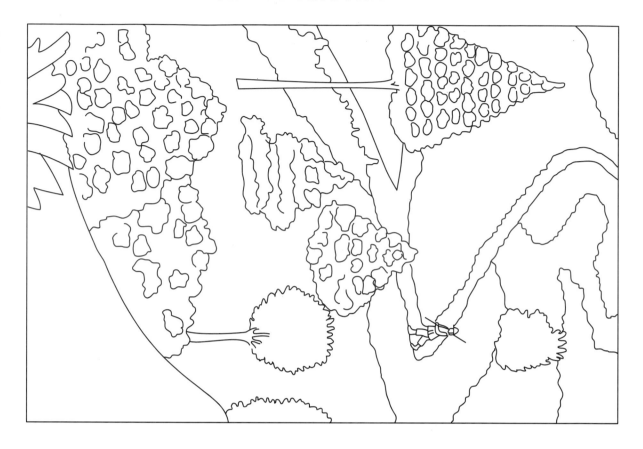

Minoan Fisherman, page 22

Grisaille Lunette, page 106

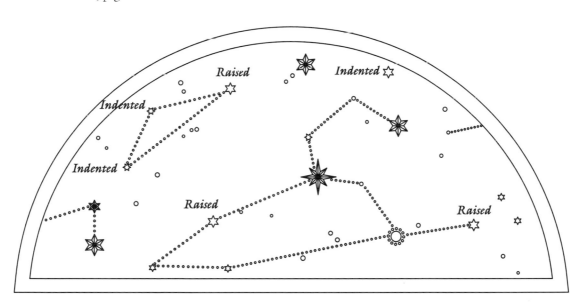

Stars Lunette, page 110. (Please note that the raised and indented stars are shown for position only; their size will depend on the moulds used.)

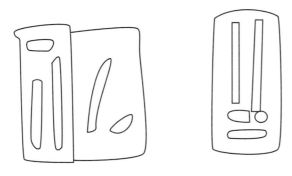

Abstract Panel, page 62

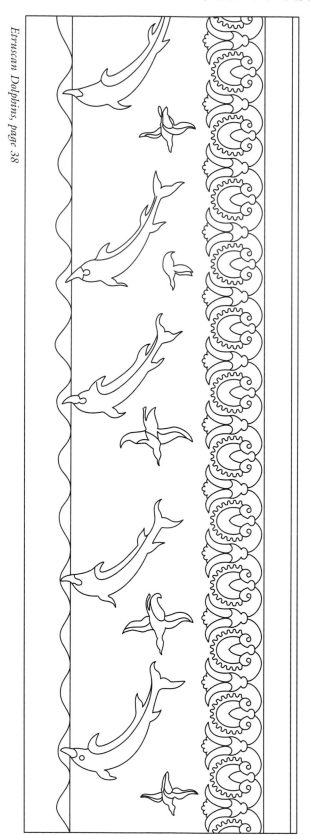

Etruscan Dolphins, page 38

Inlaid Still Life, page 76

Peach and Vase, page 56

Sgraffito Bird, page 26

Border of Lemons, page 30

Geometric Relief, page 72

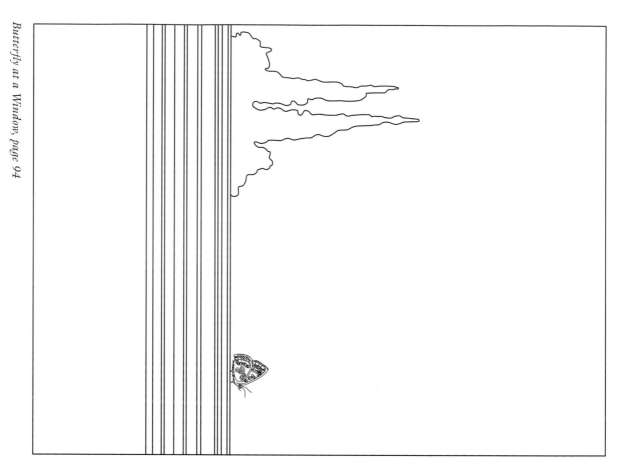

Butterfly at a Window, page 94

Tiger, page 122

LIST OF SUPPLIERS

A good local art and crafts shop will generally be able to supply most of the materials you need. Lime putty can be purchased from some art shops and specialised builders' merchants. You might also like to contact the following companies, some of whom will supply materials by mail order.

General art materials
L. Cornelissen & Son Ltd,
105 Great Russell Street, London WC1B 3RY
Tel: 0171-636 1045
Suppliers of a wide range of art materials, brushes, etc., including pigments. Mail order.

Pigments
A.P. Fitzpatrick Fine Art Materials,
142 Cambridge Heath Road, London E1 5QJ
Tel: 0171-790 0884 Fax: 0171-790 0885
Very knowledgeable specialist suppliers of all pigments, including 'historic' colours from particular mines. Also stock coloured marble dusts, brushes and a wide range of other art materials. Mail order.

Lime
The Lime Centre,
Long Barn, Morestead, Winchester SO21 1LZ
Tel: 01962 713636 Fax: 01962 715350
Specialist suppliers of lime putty, including 4-year mature. Will supply mixed plaster on request. Run courses in lime rendering. Very knowledgeable about all aspects of building with lime.

Gold leaf
Stuart R. Stevenson,
68 Clerkenwell Road, London EC1M 5QA
Tel: 0171-253 1693 Fax: 0171-490 0451
Specialist suppliers of every sort of metal leaf and all gilding materials. Wide range of brushes and general art materials plus some pigments. Mail order.

Containers
Cambrian Containers,
Unit 32, Mochdre Enterprise Park,
Newtown, Powys SY16 4LE
Tel: 01686 622994
Wholesale suppliers of containers, plastic pots with lids, etc. Mail order.

SELECT BIBLIOGRAPHY

The Artist's Handbook of Materials and Techniques, Ralph Meyer, Faber and Faber, 1991 edition.
The Craftsman's Handbook, Cennino Cennini, Translated by Daniel V. Thompson Jnr, Dover Books, 1993; Yale University Press edition 1994.
Roman Painting, Roger Ling, Cambridge University Press, 1991.
The Technique of the Great Painters, A. P. Laurie, Carroll and Nicholson, 1949. (This is out of print, but worth tracking down.)

ACKNOWLEDGMENTS

I am indebted to the Centro d'Arte Dedalo, and Alberto Felici, for inspiration and information about fresco painting. Bob Bennet from the Lime Centre and the staff of A.P. Fitzpatrick, provided much valuable technical advice. Phillip Martin's help with supplying research material was invaluable.

Janet Ravenscroft has been a tireless editor who has managed to translate my obsession with sand, lime and pigment into a manageable book format. Shona Wood's thoughtful and carefully lit step and finished project photographs are, of course, essential to the book, and both she and Janet were most patient with my lengthy explanation of fresco technique!

My family has been very supportive, putting up with the dust and drama and are gradually beginning to see the point of fresco.